REMEMBERING WWII WOMEN

Linda E. Minton

Linda E. Minton

Introduction

After the publication of *WWII Heroes: We Were Just Doing Our Job*, which featured sixty-five male veterans who served during WWII, my daughter, Amy, said, "You need to write a book about women in WWII." Thus, the birth of a new WWII book was born. As I talked with many of these humble ladies, a repeated theme was - "I didn't really do anything." As conversations deepened, it became evident that they did indeed contribute to helping on the home front. The troops couldn't be moved without the ships that were built at home; the guns couldn't be fired without the ammunition that was manufactured. In addition, collections of lard, tin and paper that were used to produce other goods for the military.

Women went to the USO facilities to entertain and comfort the military men and women. Red Cross workers were primarily female. Women and children sold war bonds to support the war costs. Many women joined the work force to build war equipment, uniforms, bullets and many other items needed to win the war and bring their men home again.

Due to the rationing of many food items, women had to be creative when cooking meals; due to the shortage of material, women made clothes for their children by using empty flour and feed sacks. They collected tin cans to use for the war needs. New cars and new refrigerators were not being produced because the steel was used for tanks and ships. Families had to do without, so the soldiers could have what they needed to win the war.

Women wanted to help with the war effort during WWII. According to www.history.com, "During World War II, 350,000 women served in the U.S. Armed Forces, both at home and abroad." Women service personnel filled the jobs that servicemen had held previously. "By 1945, there were more than 100,000 WACs and 6,000 female officers." Women were an integral part of the war effort during WWII. Fifty-five women were interviewed, and their inspiring stories are included in this book.

Table of Contents

WOMEN IN THE MILITARY

World War Two Women

"The women in WWII, more than any other women since, joined the military because they felt that our country needed them, and they wanted to be a part of protecting our nation. This all came because of Pearl Harbor. We were attacked, and so there was a very strong feeling of saving our nation – protecting our nation. Their military service meant something to them. For many of the years since, women went in the military for a variety of reasons. For many, it was to get away from home or to get an education. It wasn't to save our nation to the degree that it was in WWII."

"The Women in Military Service For America Memorial was basically built because of the WWII women. They were at a time in their life where they were looking back with pride at what they did in WWII. Their service had become far more important to them than it was the day they got out of the military at the end of the war. It became something that they wanted their children, grandchildren, and future generations to know that they served in WWII. They loved this country, and they were proud they had served to preserve it."

-Brigadier General Wilma L. Vaught, USAF, Retired

Photo by: Donna Parry

Brigadier General Wilma L. Vaught, USAF, Retired Supporter, Fundraiser, and President Emeritus, Women in Military Service For America Memorial Foundation, Washington D.C.

At the time of her retirement, one of the most highly decorated military women in the United States. General Wilma L. Vaught was the first woman to deploy with an Air Force bomb wing, and the first woman to reach the rank of brigadier general in the comptroller career field. In 1985, she retired from the military after nearly twenty-nine years of service.

Mildred Jane Baessler Doyle

What was your job or position in the WASP?

"I worked out of the engineering hangar at Freeman Field, in Seymour, Indiana, as a test pilot. We took the planes up when one of the cadets complained of a problem with the plane or after maintenance and engine change. There were three of us WASPs who were working together. Sometimes we had to pick up supplies from other fields nearby. We didn't fly in combat, and we didn't go out of the United States."

"General "Hap" Arnold wanted women to be part of the military. In June 1944, Congress voted that the WASPs were not going to be part of the military. They had to disband the program in December 1944. In December the WASP program was disbanded; I received orders to go to Panama City, Florida. So instead of going to Panama City and having to turn around and come back, I resigned from the program after one year of service. I got veterans status since I was in the program for a year, serving from November 1943 to October 1944."

Why did you join the WASPs?

"My brother was in the Navy, and my sister was in the Red Cross. In 1939, I was in college at Grand Rapids Junior College, when I heard about the Civilian Pilot Training Program. We didn't have many pilots in this country. President Franklin D. Roosevelt said we should be training civilian pilots (CPT program). It was a good opportunity to help the country too. When I went to the University of Michigan, I couldn't get in the advanced training program because it was being phased out. When I first heard about it, it was to ferry planes, and by the time I went through training, we were doing everything. They needed people for test pilot, navigator, and different things. When the opportunity to get the extra flight training was available, I joined the Civil Air Patrol. When I was in college, I received a notice asking if I would be interested in joining the WASPs. I went through seven months training in Sweetwater, Texas. When I graduated from the training program, I was assigned to Freeman Field in Seymour, Indiana. After I was released from the program, I flew some for about a year. Then it was expensive, and I had a family."

How did WWII affect your life?

"The only way it affected my life, and about everyone, was the rationing. In the summer of 1942, I worked at Hoover Manufacturing, a defense plant, as an inspector in Ann Arbor, Michigan. My job was to inspect the anvils that set off torpedoes; the anvils were located on the head of the torpedo. A lot of my friends were in the service. When I first went there to work, I saw all these women working so hard. It was production work, so you got paid by the amount you produced."

"By the end of the summer when I left, I was working just as fast too. It was interesting working there. After I graduated from college, I didn't go into the WASPs until November. In 1943, I worked with a couple fellows who had come back from the Flying Tigers. They started a company in Ann Arbor, Michigan that had a defense contract with Willow Run."

Willow Run was a defense plant that built B-24 aircraft. Because of the lack of men available, due to the war, many 'Rosie the Riveters' were hired to work at the plant. "We were doing drawings for bombers - B-24 break down drawings. I had to get released from this defense job to go into the WASPs. Yankee Air Force has a museum there now."

"My brother was on a destroyer out in the Pacific, and my sister's husband was in Patton's army in Europe. There was concern about their safety and things that were happening."

What was your greatest regret about your time in the WASP?

"I didn't have any regrets. I was glad to have the opportunity to do it. In some places there was discrimination against women, but not where I was in Freeman Field. The other two girls who had gone before me had to rent a place in town because there were no facilities for women; because we were civilians. However, when I got there the commanding officer said I could live in the nurses' quarters right on the field. I was well treated and had no problems with discrimination."

Freeman Field

Freeman Field, located in Seymour, Indiana, is approximately sixty miles south of Indianapolis, Indiana. Freeman Field, built in December 1942 and deactivated in 1948, was used as a twin-engine pilot training school. There were reported issues with black officers in the program. Freeman Field trained a group of Tuskegee Airmen and some black aviators who wanted to be pilots. The airfield held many German and Japanese aircraft after the war. Enemy planes were sent to Freeman Field, so they could be assessed by United States engineers and pilots. "It is a commercial field now and all the military buildings are gone."

What is your greatest achievement in life?

"I got married in the summer of 1944 to Donald Doyle, my check pilot. He was an instructor and after so many hours, you had to be checked to make sure you were doing everything right. He checked out the students. My daughter was born in December 1945. He was sent to Japan, and after he came back, we moved to Grand Rapids, Michigan, and had four more children. Donald was called back in the service during the Korean War. We lived in Rapid City, South Dakota, during this time."

What do you want America to know about your experiences during WWII?

"That we were doing a job to relieve the men for combat. As civilians we had to pay our own way, but we could get a salary as a civil service employee. It was a time that just about everyone was doing something. I just felt like this was something I could do to help the country. We weren't recognized afterward; we just went back home and started doing the regular things. We didn't talk about it. The things that I did my kids never heard about."

Jane was finally recognized for her service to the country by receiving the Congressional Gold Medal, the highest honor awarded to a civilian. Jane and over a thousand other WASPs were given the medals for their service to America. "We got the gold medal in 2010."

Pearl Wright Donnelly

How did WWII affect your life?

"It wasn't good. It was all right while I was in the military. On December 19, 1945, I went to Indian Town Gap, Pennsylvania, with some of the girls that I had worked with in the Air Force (Army Air Corps). We met some of the German prisoners of war. They were very nice people. They waited on us like we were princesses. One of the German prisoners said he was going to come back to the United States after the war and marry an American woman. I always wondered if he did."

What was your job or position?

"I was a cook in the Air Force (Army Air Corps). There were three of us who worked together on a shift, and we had two shifts to work. Some of the girls had gone to Cook and Bakers School, but I didn't. I already knew how to cook."

"In March 1942, I went to boot camp at Fort Oglethorpe, Georgia, for my training. During our boot camp training, the military put us through the gas chamber. We had on gas masks, but halfway through we had to take off our masks and run. The gas smelled terrible, and it was done to make us understand what we might have to go through. When we got shots, we were in a line where the medical staff shot you on both arms. I was there for six weeks – marching every day."

"We were sent to a staging area to wait for orders. Then we were sent out to the field at Fort Bragg, North Carolina. Pope Field was the training area. They put you wherever they needed you. This was a new company, and we had to clean up everything. They just built the building and left it. We had to cook on coal burning stoves. We had three large stoves, and nobody knew how to build a fire in them, but me. Where I lived was coal mining country, and I had built fires in our coal stoves at home."

"After a while, we had a major who came in and talked to us and walked around. He looked around and stayed for lunch every day. We didn't ask him what he was doing because we weren't allowed to do that. Finally, he came in one day and said, 'I have watched you long enough. You are getting an electric stove.' He came from the quartermaster. He got a steamtable for us too. Oh, we were in heaven. When we started cooking, there were only about thirteen people. They kept sending more and more, until we had about seventy people to feed by the time we left."

"They had a colonel there who didn't want us. He did not want us, but we were there for two years. After two years, he didn't want us to leave. Of course, he couldn't do anything about it because orders came from D.C."

"After that, we were sent by train to Blytheville, Arkansas. That was one of the worst places I ever went because there was nothing there. Some people asked me if I went overseas, and I said, 'I went to God's country.' They said, 'what do you mean?' I said, 'Nobody, but God would have it.' In Pope Field, we had everything; Blytheville, Arkansas, we had nothing. We worked in the hospital, because that's where the cooks had to work. We cooked for the wounded veterans, nobody else. Before we arrived, all the cooks were males. One of the guys was on the shift that I was on didn't like me at first, but I won him over by asking him to help me do things."

"We were at Blytheville, Arkansas, for several months, and then they sent us to Stout Field in Indianapolis. That was my last base; I stayed there until I was discharged in 1945 when the war ended. We went to Fort Dix, New Jersey, for separation. After I came home from the war, I began working at RCA in Indianapolis, Indiana."

Why did you join the military?

"My birth mother died when I was eight years old. So, I was

raised by an aunt and uncle. When I was twenty-two years old, I was living in Williamson, West Virginia. However, I was living with my older sister, Marie, just before I went into the military. I thought about going to Glen L. Martin, in Baltimore, Maryland to work on airplanes. I took a course to work on planes. I had to decide if I wanted to work on planes or go into the Army. So, I decided to go into the Army. We were the WAAC at that time. Six months later, we became the WAC. I joined the military and was in the (Army Air Corps) Air Force for a total of three years."

"At the time, I had a fiancé who was drafted into the Army. He wasn't the one that I married. That romance didn't last, after we returned from the military. He worked for the Norfolk & Western Railroad. He wanted me to go back to West Virginia, and I didn't want to do that. The man that I married, Carl, was in the military too. He was a good man."

Cooking in the military~

"There was a girl from Boston who wanted to come in and cook. We had to show her how to cook. Actually, she stayed in with me all the time I was in the service. I got to know people in the motor pool because we went to pick up our rations each day. We had a large cookbook that contained what we were to pick up every day. After a while, the other shifts said, 'I'll work for you if you will go pick up our rations,' I got to know some of the men, and I would get some things that were not on our lists. None of the girls liked lamb, so I asked the guys at the pick-up place if I could have beef instead of lamb. They would give it to me, if they had it."

"One time I decided that I would barbeque the lamb that I had to cook. A friend of mine came in for breakfast as well as lunch and dinner. Ann Driscoll and I were good friends. I said, 'Driscoll, how did you like your lunch today? Your meat?' She said, 'it was delicious.' I said, 'you know you ate lamb today.' She said, 'Oh, Wright, I am going to kill you.' I had her eating lamb for the first time."

What is an unexpected or funny event that you recall?

"One day we made potato salad. We used a very large bowl; you could sit in it and take a bath. It was so big you could almost swim in it. Nobody wanted to mix the potato salad. You put everything in this bowl, and there weren't any utensils that would fit under all those potatoes to mix it up. I said, 'I'll go wash my hands and arms and mix the potato salad with my hands.' After getting my hands and arms into the mixture, I couldn't get my hands out. They had to pull me out of the potato salad. Everybody was laughing and wishing they had a camera to take my picture. They never let me forget that."

Traveling with friends~

"Sometimes my friend and I would find a flight home, oftentimes, not knowing how we were going to get back. We would have been in big trouble if we hadn't gotten back to base. The crew of the plane couldn't put us on the log, and if something had happened to the plane, no one would have known where we were. Once she and I went to West Virginia to visit my sister. We had to change buses twice before we got there."

What is your greatest regret about your time in the military?

"I don't have any regrets."

What was your greatest achievement in your life?

"My greatest achievement was my marriage to Carl and my children. I have two daughters and grandchildren. I met Carl, a fireman, when I went to vote at the fire station."

How did you and your fellow women soldiers pave the way for today's women in the military?

"There were some women you could look up to and some you couldn't. Some of them mixed wrongly with the soldiers. They gave the WACs a bad name. It was women like that who ruined the name. People are going to make their own decisions about it. We had good and bad; we had more good ones than bad ones."

What do you want America to know about your experiences?

"I don't know. People are going to make up their own minds anyway. I'm glad I joined the military. It is one of the best things I ever did. If I hadn't gone into the military, I would have stayed in West Virginia. There weren't any opportunities there, and it changed my life completely."

Pearl can still wear her WWII uniform after more than seventy years.

Vera Nuckols

Why did you join the military?

Vera had a boyfriend who was later her husband, Chester
 Nuckols. "Chester was drafted in
the Army and just hated it. He
hated every part of it because it
took him away from a good paying
job." Vera thought she should do
something for the war, so weighing
only 106 pounds, Vera went in to
give blood. 'The nurse said, 'You
can't give blood.' So, I went out to
Ft. Harrison and enlisted. "I had no
problem enlisting." said Vera. Vera
enlisted in the WAAC (Women's
Army Auxiliary Corps) on February
18, 1943, and re-enlisted in the (WAC) Women's Army Corps)
on August 25, 1943. She did her basic training at Ft.
Oglethorpe, Georgia. She went to Cooks and Bakers School
and Mess Sergeants School at the base. Chester was not
very happy about Vera's joining the Army and told her not to
go overseas.

Vera's brother was also in the service. Vera's brother had
been in the CCC camp. Many young men worked in the
Civilian Conservation Camp, a work program started by the
government to help young men and to build projects that
might help the economy, to earn money during the
Depression. "Chester was sent to Germany but developed
the mumps and returned to San Diego, California. He drove
an ambulance in Washington state for a while and was later
discharged at Ft. Hood, Texas."

What was your job and position?

"When the full company arrived in Stuttgart, Arkansas, we opened our own mess with four cooks. I had the responsibility of ordering all the food, preparing the menu for each day, overseeing the operation of the kitchen, and checking the K.P.'s duties. Sometimes I would cut up sides of beef. The worst job we had was cleaning the grease pits."

What is a funny or unusual event that you recall?

"Chester sent his allotment checks to me every month, and I spent it on a set of silverware. I bought a setting every month until I had a complete set. It was International Silver, and my youngest daughter has it now. We saved until we had money to buy what we wanted."

What was your greatest regret about your time in the military?

"I have no regrets. I wish I had more time in the military. I would have had more time, but Chester came to see me during my time in Arkansas. He arrived in Stuttgart, and we were married in the post chapel there." Chester and Vera were married on May 21, 1944, three days after Vera's twenty-fourth birthday. "We were married for sixty-four years."

How did being in the military affect your life?

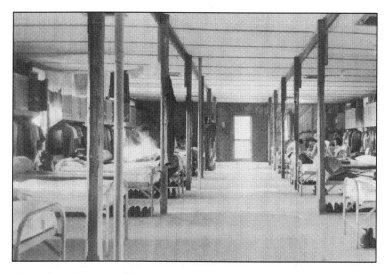

"It disturbed your lifestyle. You had to follow the rules about everything. It wasn't hard for me to accept, but that wasn't the same for everybody. I met some very nice people, and I got along with everybody. We had a company of about one hundred twenty-five women. Our barracks were built in a rice field, and we had to sleep under mosquito nets at night. The ground was saturated with water, and mosquitoes grew like horses!"

Were there any rules that women had trouble obeying?

"Well, at that time, Stuttgart, Arkansas, was the Duck Hunting Capital of the World. They had one hotel in town. We weren't allowed off base during duck hunting season because there were so many men there. We had very few women who would break any rules. We had women who worked on the planes and other jobs on base. It was a flight training school. There was a photo studio where they took pictures for various reasons."

"However, there was one girl who used to go out on Saturday night and would come back under the influence. The next morning, you never knew if she would get the eggs in the skillet or not! She was the only one that didn't obey the rules."

What do you want America to know about your experience?

Vera ordered whatever she wanted from the commissary. "We had good food. Sometimes I would cut up sides of beef. We had a freezer so when we had enough steaks on hand, I would let the girls invite friends for lunch usually on Sundays. Meat was hard to get for civilians, so the girls were always glad to come back from leave because we were never rationed. Some of the girls dated the cadets."

"When the government closed the field, the military started moving the girls to different posts. I was one of the last to leave, so I was sent to Spence Field, Moultrie, Georgia. There was a larger company of WACs there, and the work was the same. During the fall of 1945, the WACs with enough points could return to civilian life, and most of our company did that. On November 24, 1945, I was discharged from Ft. Sheridan, Illinois, which was three months before Chester was discharged."

What was your greatest achievement in your life?

"My family is my greatest achievement. I have a great family. We have two daughters, six grandchildren, and five great-grandchildren. Chester and I worked hard and everything turned out all right."

How did you and your fellow women soldiers pave the way for today's women in the military?

"The way women are now is very different from the way we were. We were just grass roots. We were there and bound to do what we were supposed to do. I have met a lot of women, including my best friend, since I became a civilian, and they said they wished they had gone in (to the military). It was a time that you were spellbound, and you had to do what they told you to do."

"One of my greatest moments was going to the Women's Memorial in Arlington National Cemetery on opening day in 1997. One room is the state room where each state sent a flag." Vera was proud that she went on the Indy Honor Flight April 5, 2014. She has attended nearly all the Indy Honor Flight homecomings for those veterans returning from their flights. One of the highlights of her trip to Washington D.C. was meeting retired Senator Bob Dole and his wife, Elizabeth.

What did you do after the war?

After Vera and Chester returned to civilian life, they lived in Evansville, Indiana, and later in Indianapolis, Indiana. She worked nineteen years at RCA where she had worked before the war. Then she went to Naval Avionics Facility to work until she retired. "I was able to retire with twenty years retirement with the years from the military."

"Veterans could eat free one night a week at this little restaurant on Washington Street. So, we took our discharge papers in and ate free." Vera ended her story by saying, "I was always glad that I went in the Army, but Chester didn't care. I have no regrets."

Ruth Talmage Wood

"In May 1942, nearly twenty-years old, I joined the WAAC and did six-month basic training. I was in the service for three years and three months. While I was in the service, they called me "Pee Wee." I was the shortest and the youngest in my group – that's how I got the name. When we first started, we were the auxiliary, or WAAC, Women's Army Auxiliary Corps, for six-months, and I was at Fort Oglethorpe, Georgia, for my basic training. The WAAC changed over to the Army, and we were known as WAC, Women's Army Corps. When we first went in, the Army didn't have things to supply us. We were given men's coveralls, and that was what we wore during our training and parades."

"Then we moved to Ft. Devins, Massachusetts, where we had our training, as far as the mechanics and things. We learned what was called second echelon. Then we moved to our station, Ft. Williams, Maine. The military disbanded all the buildings. It was strange to see just land when I returned to Ft. Williams on our twenty-fifth anniversary." Ft. Williams was officially closed in 1962, and sold to the town of Cape Elizabeth, Maine, in 1964. The residents of Cape Elizabeth voted to make the area that served as the Harbor Defenses of Portland during WWII into a park.

What was your job or position in the military?

"I was a corporal in the motor pool and my job was to transport the officer's children to school in Portland, Maine. Also, my job was driving the mess sergeant for the officer's mess. We would pick up any supplies that they wanted, so it was quite an adventure every day to go to all the stores. My other job in the military was handling the mail which I did in civilian life, before and after the war. I left General Motors to go to the military and returned to General Motors after the war ended."

Why did you join the military?

"At the time, it was right after Pearl Harbor, and my brother, Harold Talmage, was in Pearl Harbor at the time of the attack. He was stationed aboard the USS *Whitney* which was in the bay area." The USS *Whitney* fired at enemy and American planes (accidentally) and helped other ships in need after the attack was over. "It was a couple weeks before we heard that he was all right. It was very stressful. Many things came up in my civilian life that I thought – I'm single, I'm free, why not? Anyway, I enjoyed my duty. It was good companionship with everybody. There were over two hundred in our barrack area; we had quite a group of girls. We had a first sergeant that was little, but she was mighty. When she spoke, you listened."

What did your parents think about you joining the military?

"Well, mother was very disturbed. She didn't want me to go in (the military) and go overseas. She made me promise not to volunteer to go overseas. She knew if I was sent overseas, that would be it. I didn't volunteer, but in 1945, when they declared the war over, I had a chance to go overseas. After making the promise to mom, I thought maybe I should just go home."

What is your greatest regret about your time in the military?

"I thought my greatest regret was being away from home. I was a homebody. My brother, Harold, was in the Navy and my sister was at home, and I just missed my family."

What was an unexpected or funny event that you recall?

"We used to go on the coast line at Kennebunk to collect clams and have a clambake. In previous times, we had collected many clams, but this one time we went at the wrong time. We didn't find any at all which disappointed the military people. Another time, we went to Chattanooga, Tennessee, in a convoy of jeeps and trucks. I had a chance to be in command, so I drove the jeep back and forth down the line of vehicles to keep them in shape. It was quite an experience. I basically drove a jeep most of the time."

How did WWII affect your life?

"It actually took me away from my family, but it made me grow up and realize there were other people other than yourself. Before (the military), I was just young and sowing my oats. I was always interested in automobiles and always had a car that I would repair myself. It helped me to be interested in how to do things on cars. I guess that's why I went into the motor pool. The military looked at your background and tried to place you where you fit."

"The rationing – when I came home, I had to have rationing coupons to get gas, and that slowed me down! I didn't care for that. I had a 1935 or 1936 Chevy coupe before the war, which I drove back and forth to school and to my part time job at General Motors. After the war, I had a 1946 or 1947 Chevy coupe."

How had life changed since you left home?

"Mother had gotten older, and they were thinking of moving up north. That really changed my situation. My older sister was married, so that left me up on the high limb. It was a quite a change; as you grow you get used to things like that."

"In 1952, I met my husband, Elgan "Roy" Wood, by accident when having a picnic. I went canoeing with some friends, and we paddled over two or three lakes that day." After Ruth met Roy, they spent many times canoeing together. They were married in 1954. Ruth and Roy moved to a lake where many fond memories were made with that same canoe. "Today it is enjoyed by my children, grandchildren and great-grandchildren."

What do you want America to know about your experiences?

"I would like for America to know that I was extending myself as far as learning new things. I always liked to read and do new things."

How did you and your fellow women soldiers pave the way for today's women in the military?

"They have learned many things from the older women, such as commanding and taking of orders."

What was your greatest achievement in your life?

"My greatest achievement was my family. I had three children and a step-daughter, and I was strict; they had to be honest, loving, and courteous to older people. I am very proud of my children. They are exceptional when it comes to manners." These traits are evident in Ruth as well.

Booth, Mildred "M.J."

Mildred, nicknamed M.J., was able to fit into her U.S. Navy uniform that she wore during her military service over seventy years ago. It fit her perfectly!

"I enlisted in the Navy WAVE program, attended Hunter College, and Oklahoma A & M. and then served as a Yeoman in Florida. The Navy sent me through business school, and I graduated down in Oklahoma. Then I got married. I went to Florida to an air base where they had very large planes that flew to Hawaii and South America. I worked in Navy personnel at Ope-Ioda Naval Air Station near Miami, Florida." There were many military bases in south Florida. According to the website, Florida Memory, "Dozens of military bases were established or expanded in the state."

What was your job or position in the military?

"I was in charge of Navy personnel or the discharge person."

Why did you join the military?

"I graduated from high school, and it was the thing to do. My friends said, 'Why don't you join the Navy.' I thought, 'The Navy will never take me.' But they took me. I went to New York and got my basic training."

How did WWII affect your life?

"I met my future husband, Bud, in the sixth grade, but never  actually dated him until he came home on leave in World War II with his new, shiny pilot's wings. Howard, or Bud, enlisted at age eighteen in the Army Air Corps and was in the Fifth Air Force. After we were married, my husband went back to college at Syracuse University to get his degree. Then we went up near Boston, Massachusetts, to live for six years. I traveled a lot with my husband, both in the military and with his firm."

Later in life, M.J.'s son was a helicopter pilot.

"I was so young and so pretty." M.J. said teasingly.

What do you want America to know about your WWII experiences?

"I can't say that I have done very much. It was a good way for me to see the world. When WWII ended, I was living in Oklahoma at that time."

Eunice Desjardins

Do you remember the beginning of the war?

"When the Japanese attacked Pearl Harbor on December 7, 1941, I was working as a secretary in Concord, New Hampshire, and rooming with an elderly couple. Their young grandson, who had just been commissioned as an ensign after graduating from Annapolis, was killed in that attack, and it nearly killed his grandfather. That started my thinking about what my future might be in the war that was declared the next day."

How did WWII affect your life?

"Soon after that, my grandfather died, and my father had to combine his small meat market with my grandfather's large general store just down the street. Because of the complicated bookkeeping, caused by everyone having to use government coupons to purchase food, gasoline, and other goods—all of which were sold at the general store my father urged me to come home from Concord to help him. I had worked at that store all through my high school years. So, I spent the next three years back in the tiny village of Campton, New Hampshire."

"While I was there, I worked with the Red Cross and volunteered to spend time each week at a local lookout station watching planes flying overhead and identifying them before calling a government center to report them. If foreign planes attacked our country, it was thought that they would fly over our area first."

"Everyone in the United States worked towards a common goal and saved everything we could, including every bit of string, bacon grease, and paper all of which we contributed to the war effort."

"After three years helping my father, I felt I could leave to enlist. I chose the Navy because my girlfriend had been among the first to enlist in the WAVES, and she was encouraging me. So, on July 13, 1944, along with many other young women, I arrived at Grand Central Station, New York City, and was driven to WAVES boot camp at Hunter College in the Bronx, New York City. The government had completely taken over the college, as well as two large apartment houses nearby."

"For the next six weeks this would be our home. Twelve of us were to be in an apartment intended for two people and with only one bathroom. Looking back on it, I can only imagine how we all managed to get ready in full uniform and march to an early breakfast."

"We were then taken to another building to be fitted with our uniforms. They were navy blue suits to wear all year and grey and white striped seersucker for summer only. Later we had the option of buying white sharkskin suits for dress. All our clothes were well designed and fit well. We were issued a very heavyweight Navy winter coat and shoes. All our civilian clothes were then immediately shipped back home."

"When our platoon marched to the big regimental review field to join many other platoons for periodic inspections, we ended up standing at parade rest for long periods as we waited for several thousand more to arrive at their positions. It was extremely hot in New York City in July and many girls fainted, but we could not help them and that was hard. Other personnel were sent in to rescue them."

"Our boot camp, as a whole, wasn't nearly as difficult as it is today. We were needed to serve just as quickly as possible, so our training there was some exercise, but mostly learning Navy rules/regulations, who to salute and when, and lots of marching. Also, we were interviewed to determine where we would go from there. We didn't have the same rugged boot camp that the services have today. If we had a trade or training already, they took advantage of our training requiring less time at advanced training, so I was sent to Iowa State Teachers College in Cedar Falls, Iowa."

"Since troop trains were being threatened at that time, we went from New York City to Cedar Falls by way of Canada. We were aboard an old coal burning train with windows wide open, so we were a sorry looking bunch when we arrived. The train was so long that when we arrived at our destination, the train car I was on unloaded in a cornfield. From then on everything was much better than boot camp: great food, only four girls to a dormitory and bathroom, interesting studies, and recreational options. We were marching on a beautiful campus singing along with music from the campanile tower. I arrived there the middle of August and went home for Thanksgiving leave before going to my permanent assignment."

What was your job or position?

"I was assigned to the Legal Section of the Bureau of Ordinance where I served as a legal secretary for one lawyer, and he was a very nice man; so, it was a pleasant situation and a great experience. I was one of about 30,000 service women in the District of Columbia. Since WAVES were being assigned there faster than housing for them could be built, we were moved several times. I think I was in Quarters D three times, Quarters K in Virginia once, and also one winter in the Mayflower Hotel which the Navy had taken over. There were never enough public buses; however, since we were always in uniform, the local citizens were great about offering us a ride to work and again back to the barracks at night. Since it was a long commute to work each morning and back to our barracks at night, we didn't have much time for recreation, and our evenings were usually spent writing letters home, laundering our clothes, and keeping our belongings ready for surprise inspections."

"Our name WAVES stood for Women Accepted for Volunteer Emergency Services, and it was originally planned that we would be discharged after the end of the war as soon as our particular job was no longer needed. So, in my case, as soon as my lawyer's work was completed, I would go home. However, after about half of the WAVES had been separated, management decided that they were going to permanently need women in the Navy, so we could have stayed in. However, I planned to get married in a couple months, so I wasn't interested. Since then, women have become member of the regular Navy and eventually began to be promoted the same as the men."

Did you meet any celebrities during your time in the service?

"President Franklin Delano Roosevelt's wife, Eleanor, came to WAVE Quarters D once to speak to us, and although she stood right next to me at one point, I wasn't introduced to her. She was very influential and powerful and was given credit for the beginning of African Americans being allowed to ride at the front of the bus while in D.C. However, when the bus crossed the line into Virginia, they still had to move to the back of the bus."

Why did you join the WAVES?

"When I felt the time had come when I could in good conscience stop helping my father in his store, I was anxious to do more to serve my country, and there were posters everywhere saying how much women were needed to replace stateside jobs currently filled by Navy men, so that they could go overseas for combat. I had a girlfriend who had been one of the first volunteers for WAVES officers training having just graduated from college. She was very enthusiastic about the WAVES and encouraged me to volunteer. I went to Boston, Massachusetts, volunteered and reported for duty in July 1944, at the age of twenty-three."

What do you remember the end of the war?

"The most memorable day, of course, was V-J Day. When we got the news that the war was finally over and that the boys would be coming home, we just poured out of the buildings to celebrate. Traffic was stopped and completely clogging the roads, so young folks just ran from one car top to the next hugging, sharing drinks, kissing, and shouting. We each had special reasons to be so excited. We had the rest of the week off work, and it was a constant celebration. I just discovered my only letter home that my folks had kept was about V-J day and all that weekend."

What is your greatest achievement in life?

"That question is a hard one as no one has ever asked me that before. Being stationed in D.C. changed my life and set the path for the rest of it. While in D.C., I was invited by three friends to visit them where they were working at a government facility in Mt. Weather, Virginia, about an hour and a half bus ride south of D.C. It was there I met my future husband, Robert "Bob" Cooper. He visited me in D.C. several times while he was still at Mt. Weather before returning to his parents' home in Muncie, Indiana. Except for the two times I visited him at his parents' home, our courting was done through correspondence. We were married on June 16, 1946. He was a wonderful man and probably my biggest achievement was helping create a happy home and bearing two great children, a son and a daughter. Unfortunately, after just twelve wonderful years, Bob got multiple sclerosis and died six years later, Eventually, I married Joseph Desjardins and that also was a happy marriage. I am close to my two stepdaughters and my stepson. I have been very blessed!"

What do you want America to know about your experiences?

"I am very grateful for the experience as it taught me so

 much about life: self-reliance, to do the very best I could in every situation, to step out boldly and make the best of whatever happens, and to always remember that we 'win some and lose some' as we go through life. To do well in service now, a young woman would need to be able to complete a more difficult boot camp and face different challenges; however, it can offer a very good experience and future."

Eunice at Annapolis, Md

After the war~

"When I married Bob a couple of months after being discharged from the WAVES, I moved to Muncie, Indiana, his hometown. Later we lived in Pendleton, Winchester, and Fort Wayne, Indiana. Joe and I lived in Indianapolis, eventually retiring to Ogunquit, Maine. After thirty-five years enjoying life at this 'beautiful place by the sea' in the fall of 2015, I moved back to Indianapolis to live with my daughter and her husband."

"Special flights to Washington D.C. are provided for veterans to see all the war memorials, and I made that trip on April 1, 2017. This outing provided by the Indy Honor Flight organization is a wonderful gift free for veterans. I had seen all the memorials before but somehow had missed seeing the Tomb of the Unknown, so that was very exciting for me. Being the oldest veteran and the only woman veteran on our plane, I felt that I was representing all WAVES. Many service women thanked me for being in the group who had broken the ground for them."

Hellen Holder Guthrie

What was your job or position in the Navy?

"I was a Specialist Q First Class in the U.S. Navy in Intelligence as a WAVE. I enlisted in August 1943 and was sent to Hunter College in the Bronx. My job was as a cryptographer in the Japanese section. We worked seven to three, the next week three to eleven, and the following week eleven to seven; it just rotated. After my training, it was a wonderful time to be in Washington D.C. There was so much going on, and you got to meet so many people. It was an experience that you never forget, and it was something that I was very happy that I did. It was interesting."

"The messages that had been intercepted were brought in with the Japanese encryption. They were encrypted at least three times. They had already been translated once. Then they had to be translated again in the machine. We typed it up and then that was as far as we went with the messages before they went to the next group. They figured out A means B, and so on. The Russian's messages were decoded on big machines, and when they were going the floor would vibrate. Americans were working on these messages. There was never a week went by that some of the officers' quarters didn't get ransacked when they were trying to find out what we knew or what we were working on. We couldn't say anything to our family. We did not talk to anybody. I usually said, 'When the commander wants a letter, I type it for him,' which was true."

When did you join the Navy?

"I joined in August 1943. The WAVES were organized in 1942 to relieve men of the secretarial jobs, so they could serve in combat jobs. This was the first time there had been women in the Navy except for Navy nurses. I was probably in the fourth or fifth class of WAVES. I don't know exactly how many there were at that time. There were classes of approximately four hundred, and I went to Hunter College in the Bronx, New York." According to Homefront Heroines website, "Approximately 100,000 women were accepted into the Navy as WAVES. The Navy established a rigorous screening and training process designed to weed out women who didn't meet the Navy's high standards."

"After the apprenticeship there, we were sent to other schools. I had always been a secretary to a lawyer. So, I went to yeoman school which was a secretarial and office school. This school was on the college campus of Oklahoma A & M. When we finished school, we were deployed to wherever we were needed around the country. There was no way a woman in the Navy could go outside the continental United States. We wore dresses, not pants."

"The Specialist Q group was a new group which was just formed. After my training, I was waiting to hear my name called. After many names were called and my name was not among them, I thought, am I just going to stay here? Then it was announced, 'we are taking the top ten percent of this class and sending them to Washington to be cryptographers and to be Specialist Q's.' So, I am sitting there, and 'what in the world am I going to do? I don't even work crossword puzzles.' The Navy shipped us off to Washington, where they had just built a brand-new WAVE quarters across from a former private girl's school."

"In this building, the Japanese decoded messages were housed on the second floor, and the Russian decoders were on the first floor. Everything except the building was new, and we lived just across the street. We had a sundeck on the top of our quarters. Every afternoon, we couldn't sleep because the planes would fly over the sundeck where the women were lying."

"When we were in the Navy for a while, the Navy asked us to move out of the building. The new recruits needed a place to live. The people of Washington D.C. were very wonderful. Everybody rented out their spare room. I was living in this house when President Franklin D. Roosevelt died in April 1945. He was lying in state in the Capitol. I was working the midnight shift, and my landlady said when I came in, 'Are you going to get in line to see President Roosevelt?' I said, 'heavens, no.' She looked at me and said, 'what!' I said, 'no.' She was absolutely floored. She could not understand why I wouldn't go down there and stand for four or five hours just to walk pass his casket. She was really put out with me."

What was an unexpected event that you recall?

"I was meeting a friend of mine at the Willard Hotel." The Willard Hotel, a famous hotel in Washington D.C., was the place where many important people met, and special political meetings took place. "I was sitting there waiting for her in the bar when this really good-looking man came in. He looked over at me and said, 'hello' and I said 'hello.' I thought he looks familiar, and he sat down one or two tables away. Finally, I remembered, 'It was Robert Taylor.' He was a lieutenant in the Navy."

"Another time, we got a pass to go to New York City at the end of our shift. If we had forty-eight hours, we could go there to visit and sightsee. There were tours and millionaires had turned over their houses for the military. There were bunkbeds and things like that we could use. We could stay at these houses at no cost. One time we wanted to go to Radio City Music Hall, and the line was around the block. The people in charge took the service people out of line to see the show. We didn't have to pay one penny. It was the same way with the ferry if you went out to Staten Island. People were wonderful to us."

"I took my first airplane ride when I was in the service. On one occasion, I had been at home and left from Indianapolis. We were practically in Cincinnati, Ohio, when they said it was going to be bumpy. It was cold, so the stewardess gave us all blankets. When the plane arrived in Cincinnati, they told the civilians to get off the plane. Only the military were left on the plane. Next, they said we are going up to Cleveland, Ohio. It was still storming, and I was worried about getting back to base by seven in the morning. I didn't want to be AWOL. We went to Philadelphia next, but it was still storming, so we couldn't land. The plane went to New York, and the weather was clear enough to continue to Washington D.C. When we arrived in Washington D.C., we were twenty minutes ahead of time."

How did WWII affect your life?

"It made it better. I had never had a chance to go places and do things." Hellen's mother and father died at a very young age, and she and her brother Gene were raised by her grandparents in Spencer, Indiana. "My grandparents thought it was a good thing for me to go into the Navy. My brother Gene was in Europe with General Patton. He had been in the Army for several years. In fact, when I was twenty-one years old, he had been in the Army for several years. He stayed in the Army for thirty-five years and retired as a colonel in the 1970's. Gene loved the Army, and he and about a dozen men developed the Patton tank. As a sergeant, he drove for General Patton; and when he was in Europe, he was a tank commander at the Battle of the Bulge. My brother thought General Patton could do no wrong."

Do you remember when the war ended?

"When the war was over in Europe, people came in and told us. 'Germany has surrendered, go out and celebrate.' A group of us went downtown Washington D.C. and joined in the celebrations down there. In 1945, when the Japanese surrendered, I don't recall that we did anything. It was sort of an ordinary day. After the war ended, I had an opportunity to sign up for four years and go to Hawaii. If I stayed in for four more years, I could go to Pearl Harbor. I thought, that's for me. I called my grandmother to tell her that I was ready to take my test and become a Navy chief. My grandmother said, 'Oh, I think that's grand.' Then there was complete silence on the phone. Followed by, 'You aren't going any place; you are coming home.' said my grandfather. So, I went home. Maybe it was for the best; maybe it wasn't." There was still sadness even after more than seventy years.

"In 1942, I met my future husband, Ralph, when my brother, Gene, brought him down to meet the family. Ralph and I were married in 1947."

What was your greatest achievement in your life?"

"My greatest achievement was probably my son. I think I have had an interesting life, especially because of the years I spent working in politics, particularly because of the people you get to meet. I met President Ronald Reagan twice. I was in charge of taking care of Nancy Reagan, and she was the nicest person you would ever meet. She was not stuck up, just as common as an old shoe. We had an event for Barbara Bush, and she was not as nice. President Ford came to make a dedication or speech, and I met him."

How did you and your fellow women soldiers pave the way for today's women in the military?

"I think we were pioneers, and we had the best of everything. For example, our accommodations, the way we were treated, and we had soldiers to sweep the floors and wash the dishes. If you met somebody, they were happy to meet you, and it was a time when women were treated like ladies."

What do you want America to know about your experiences during the war?

"It was wonderful, and I enjoyed it. I am very happy that it happened." Hellen was awarded the Sagamore of the Wabash in December 1983 for her work in politics. The Sagamore of the Wabash is awarded for outstanding service to the state by the governor of Indiana. Hellen's award was presented by Governor Robert Orr.

Norma Lewis

"I grew up in a small town in Connecticut with my aunt and uncle. They were like parents to me. They had two sons and a daughter. I call my cousins my brothers and sister because we were that close. We lived near a lake and went swimming every day. We were a happy family. None of us were expecting the country to go to war. On December 7, 1941, I was horseback-riding with my boyfriend. His family had a farm and several horses. When we started back to his house after riding, we saw his mother looking out the kitchen window sobbing into her apron. We couldn't imagine what was wrong. She quickly answered, 'It is war! We have been attacked by the Japanese at Pearl Harbor.' We asked, 'Where is Pearl Harbor?' We had never heard of it. Everyone was running around asking questions about what was going to happen now. The next day was Monday, and it seemed like all the men and boys were going to the post office to enlist. Their mothers said, 'Please don't go.'"

How did WWII affect your life?

"Everyone had to cut back on things like aluminum. Everything was for the military, so they could protect us. Everything was different; we were doing without or using something else. Whatever they told us to give up, we did. We had a little booklet with stamps in it for gas, which was used only to go to work and back. Most gasoline was for military ships and planes. We cut back on meat. There was gossip that some people still ate steak."

"Someone said, 'So-and-so would go the butcher, slip him a few dollars to buy steak, while we are buying hamburger.' People used to complain about these wealthy people."

"During World War II, women could finally go into the military. I immediately said, 'I want to go,' but I was told, 'Nice girls do not go into the military. We are not going to discuss it again.' The WAVES (Women Accepted for Volunteer Emergency Services) was established in July 1942, and my sister and I wanted to sign up. Finally, six months later, my aunt and uncle said, 'Just go if you must.'"

What was your job or position in the military?

"In July 1943, my sister Betty and I enlisted in the WAVES and were sent to New York. We spent six weeks in boot camp. We wanted to be together after boot camp. However, my sister was sent to the Baltimore, Maryland, and I went to Charleston, South Carolina. We didn't see each other again until after the war."

"I signed up to be a Control Tower Operator. When the results from my exam came back, I was told, 'You passed everything except the math, which is extremely important with bringing in planes and sending them out. You should pick another area.' Next, I applied to be a pilot with a specialty of learning how to fly in the dark. We had a mockup of a plane with a cockpit. You would pull a cover over your head, then learn how to fly blind in fog and at night. Once again, I was told I did well except I flunked math. My next choice was to be a gunnery instructor. Believe it or not, in high school, we had a rifle range. It was boys and girls, and I was a crack shooter. I remember being told, 'You were absolutely overwhelming with your performance, but math was a problem again.'"

"I was then told I would be going to a college in Iowa. I said, 'There is no water there, there is no Navy there; there is just corn in Iowa.' I was informed that I would be doing office work. I was very disappointed, not realizing that any job was important to the war effort. I stayed in Iowa for six weeks doing shorthand and typing, things I already knew. Then I received my duty station and was shipped to Charleston, South Carolina. I was in for a surprise. My superiors called me in and told me I would be in the secret service. I was never to tell my family, ever. They said if you tell your family anything, tell them you are working in the galley peeling potatoes. My family called and asked if something was wrong. They said, 'Naval officers are walking around our neighborhood, going to my church, and the high school I attended. Are you in the brig? Did you do something wrong'? I answered, 'Oh, no, I am working in the kitchen until I am assigned to do office work.'"

"One of my duties was working with submarine air search. Two months after Pearl Harbor, German U-boats torpedoed our tankers and freighters in sight of the East Coast of the United States. They boldly shot at our blimps and slow-moving convoys at night. Burning ships could be seen from Jacksonville, Florida, to Wilmington, North Carolina. We knew the Germans were out there. Our job was to keep the German subs away from our shores and drive them further out into the mid-Atlantic."

"While I was on duty in Charleston, depth charges were dropped damaging a German U-Boat. German prisoners were taken immediately to the hospital by the Coast Guard. These were the very first prisoners taken in combat by any armed forces. Because our jobs were top secret, the WAVES were never allowed to tell each other what their assignments were – including other WAVES from other units."

"Fifty years after the war ended, the men and women from our unit were invited to attend the Sixth District Intelligence Reunion to be held in Charleston, South Carolina. There, we WAVES reunited and finally revealed what our individual assignments were during our tours of duty. Sharing the information was an unforgettable, memorable experience. One WAVE worked undercover with sailors in civilian clothes. Pretending to fish, these sailors patrolled in a rowboat equipped with a two-way radio to communicate with the WAVE, who was stationed in the Sixth District Intelligence Office. Another WAVE was assigned to draw maps to scale using information from missionaries coming back from Hong Kong where the Communists had taken over."

"In another unit a WAVE typed up reports about all the rice patties and the terrain. One WAVE had the job of keeping track of all the sailors going overseas and returning. One name on a roster was not familiar to WAVE Dorothy Phillips, and she brought it to the attention of a superior. Due to her exceptional attention to detail, it was discovered a saboteur was on board. Had the WAVE not discovered his false name, the saboteur would have destroyed the ship and the entire crew." The WAVE was awarded a medal and told to put it in a safe place and to not speak of it again until the war ended. They say a woman can't keep a secret, well she did!"

Describe the German prisoners

"The German prisoners walked all over the base in Charleston. They were not going to run away because they were terrified and very young. They were not treated roughly; we didn't touch a hair on their heads. We never made eye contact when we saw them. The prisoners were guarded by Marines. The Germans were kept busy doing every kind of job – working in the galley or sweeping the base."

Where were you the day the war ended?

"The day the war ended was my day off, so I went to a movie at a local theater in Charleston with another WAVE. We suddenly heard loud yelling and people shouting in the back of the theater, but we couldn't understand what was being said. Everyone at the theater was annoyed and since the theater was dark, the movie was still being shown. After the movie ended and we left, we were stunned to see mobs of people shouting that the war was over!"

"The crowd was wild, and my WAVE friend and I were in a panic. We pushed through the crowds trying to find a way back to our barracks. We finally came to an alley and a hand reached out and grabbed my jacket and pulled us along. We couldn't get away. When we came to the end of the alley, we saw a short white-haired man telling us not to be afraid as he was going to give us a ride back to our barracks. His wife was sitting in the front seat of the car. She reassured us to not be afraid. I've never forgotten that kind couple."

Do you have any regrets?

"I have no regrets. I only know that I was proud to serve my country."

Norma, why are you wearing just the hat from your uniform?

"Because that's the only part of it that still fits!"

Anita Harris Parker

"I was born in Texas and lived there until 1941, when I moved to Fresno, California. My mother died when I was thirteen, and my dad had lost track of what I was doing.

After I joined the WAVES, I went back home to see my dad before I went to boot camp. There were several articles in the local paper about it, so I think he must have been proud of me joining the Navy."

Why did you join the military?

"I broke up with my boyfriend. Well, I was very disappointed about it, and I was looking for something to do. I worked for the telephone company in Fresno, California. I had heard a lot about the WAVES, so I checked into it. The WAVES accepted me into the military, but I had to wait a month because the telephone company was considered essential work for the war. Therefore, I waited a month before I entered the service."

What was your job or position?

"In 1943, I joined the U.S. Navy WAVES and did my basic training at Hunter College, New York. As a Seaman First Class, I worked in the Finance Office or Dispersing Office, in Pasco, Washington, and then to Hawaii. I was twenty-two years old and was assigned to two different stations in Hawaii. By the time I left, I had moved up to SKD Chief in Dispersing. These were all acting appointments, as we were not considered part of the Navy, actually. We were considered part of it, just not stationary, because I was a WAVE. I used to go to the commissary at Pearl Harbor quite often. There wasn't as much destruction as you would think about this time. Every so often you saw something that would remind you of the attack on Pearl Harbor."

"When we took money with us to pay the men at the bases, we had to carry a weapon – a 45. I didn't have to carry a gun when I was working in the office, only when we took the payroll out to the hangars."

Anita (center) and two unidentified WAVES

"One time we were sent to Johnston Island to pick up some account books. We wanted to go to Kwajalein but were unable to go to the other islands." Kwajalein, an atoll, is part of the Marshall Islands. The Battle of Kwajalein was fought from January 31 to February 3, 1944. The Allies won this battle and further pushed back the Japanese. "We didn't know we weren't to go out of the continental United States, but we had." Johnston Island, located in the Pacific Ocean southwest of Hawaii, was used for secret nuclear testing during the 1960's. "It is somewhat of a manmade island because they had to extend the island to accommodate the big planes that used to come in to land. If you came in at the wrong angle, it took your wheels off."

"It was a very interesting trip. The captain of the station went all out to entertain us."

Did you have any regrets about your time in the military?

"No, never. It was one of the most educating things that I did in my life. Actually, the military got me started on two different careers. I started singing with the band at different stations. In Hawaii, I contacted a combo that was part of the Pearl Harbor band and worked with them going around to different stations or camps entertaining the troops. Sometimes we would go to as many as two places in one afternoon. We would leave the office at 4:30 p.m., and we were allowed out until 9:00 p.m. It was good because all the fellas in the bands were from Big Bands in the states. One of Tony Pastor's recordings was, *Confessing*."

"Bob Crosby was in the audience one time. It made me a little bit nervous. I had the reputation for knowing any song that anyone requested. I don't have a favorite song; I like them all. I was exposed to music when I was in high school, then professionally in this setting. When I came home, I went to Chicago and studied music and voice professionally. I heard that there was a band in Chicago that was all military, and they needed a military singer, so that worked out for me. I worked as a vocalist with dance bands in Chicago, Phoenix, and Fresno when I came back to California. I met my first husband while I was singing in Fresno."

How did WWII affect your life?

"It affected it very much because I always had an aptitude for math and numbers. When I went through testing, everything came out numbers. So, I was sent to storekeeper school at Georgia State College for Women. I had a good background in accounting when I came out of the WAVES which is what I did all my life. That got me started on my career, and I took some more courses when I came home."

Were there any funny events that happened during this time?

"The women went out to the firing range and one of the girls was very young. Someone would shoot a round, and then we would go out and paste up the holes. The young girl shot, and there were no holes to paste up. She shot again and again no holes. The last time she shot there was one hole. We went out to paste up the hole and discovered she had shot the paste bucket full of holes. All three rounds had gone into the paste bucket. We didn't take her to the rifle range any more. I never had to fire my weapon except at the rifle range. We practiced with 38's and carried 45's. I often wondered what would happen in a hangar if we had to pull those guns out and use them. I think it would have been random shooting."

What do you want America to know about your experiences?

"I think it was a very good idea to let the women participate, and I think the military could have broadened our participation. I think they should have done that."

"There was a lot of resistance, and you felt it sometimes where we came into a certain base that they resented us. The same thing in the little towns where we lived, much like Pascal, Washington. We would go into a town close by and people resented us. I think it was the men mostly. The women thought it was great. Pascal was a desolate place."

"When I came back to California, I was discharged in San Francisco. The guys were not very nice. That was the worst that I felt."

What was your greatest achievement in your life?

"I think that raising two daughters by myself should count for something."

How did your fellow women soldiers and you pave the way for today's women in the military?

"There were some good and some bad. It broadened my opportunities and afforded me more independence. One thing that I found was that there are all kinds of people that go into the service. I was exposed to them constantly because we all lived in a barrack together, and it was an education. I didn't graduate from college, and it gave me the opportunity to get a job. I enjoyed all of it because it was new, and I got the opportunity to go to Hawaii. That was very nice because I was there about a year and a half. We had women who were officers who took interest in us. I was told many times to cut my hair. You can't have long hair."

What was it like when the war was over?

"Everyone was elated, of course. I had a brother who was in Italy in a big battle, and he came home safely."

"Everyone in camp brought out their bottles of booze that they had been hiding. We went to the Rec Hall and had a party for the rest of the night until dawn. We celebrated and were very happy about it. People wanted to get home. I didn't go home until June of 1946 because they needed accounting people to absorb all these accounts from outlying stations. The military asked us to stay over if we could.

I was enjoying myself, so I stayed. I found out if the guys needed an advance, and if you did that, you could always get doughnuts in the morning. If you were nice to them, they would be nice to you. I never had trouble getting a jeep if I wanted to go into town."

Emily Sehr

Why did you join the military?

Emily Egolf was working in a bank in Brooklyn, New York, in 1944. She was training a girl who was making more than she was. Emily said, "That made me mad." Another girl whom Emily worked with said she was going to join the Navy. Emily was off work for a few days. When she returned to work, the girl told her that she had joined the Navy. "That just killed my soul. I went home and broke the news to my parents. Of course, they didn't think it was a good idea. I went to a Recruiting Office on famous Wall Street in New York City, signed up, and went home to tell my parents. My parents were not very happy. Girls didn't go away from home. Dad had a business and wanted me to do the driving for him."

"I wanted to go to college, but my father said that girls didn't need to go to college to get married and have children. I wanted to join the Marines, but you had to have college and I didn't have any college, just a high school education."

Did your parents ever forgive you for joining the Navy?

"I don't know. I never asked them!" she said with a laugh. "But one day they put a flag in the window showing a military person from their home was in the service."

Emily, Michael (dad), and Anna (mom)

What was your job or position?

Emily was accepted into the Navy right after Thanksgiving 1944. "I didn't have to prove that I was twenty-one...I must have looked old." she said, "They told me what I needed, and I signed papers. I was to report to Hunter College in the Bronx. All the girls were very friendly. We had to go to a big fieldhouse to eat our meals. It was a lot of fun."

"We were put into companies, and that was fun even though we had to get up early in the morning. We had to be dressed and out in line when they took roll call. We practiced marching, and it was cold. We had boots and our own clothes until our uniforms were made to order. A week later, we got our navy-blue uniforms."

"We were asked to choose three things that you would like to do." Emily selected air traffic controller, typist, or IBM Keypunch operator. "I was turned down for the air traffic controller because they said I had an accent." Emily still has the Brooklyn accent even though she hasn't lived in New York City for more than seventy years. Keypunch operators worked on a machine that punched holes into rectangular cards. Information was typed into the keypunch machine which punched holes in the cards. "I didn't want anything to do with banking! So, I went into keypunching. It was new and the latest thing coming up. No one knew what a keypunch operator was at the time. We didn't either, and now it is obsolete. The whole group of forty that I went in with were put into keypunching. I went to school at the IBM school in New York City for two weeks."

What was your greatest regret about your time in the military?

"I have none. They were the best years of my life. I loved it. I was in the Navy for two years. When the war was over, the Navy released you. They gave you fifty-dollars and told you to go home. Everything was cheap in those days."

How did WWII affect your life?

"It got me out of New York! I met my husband, John, while I was in the military." Emily went on to explain, "We slept in bunks and my bunkmate, Bess, and I had been out on the town and were coming back for the night. We started talking to this bunch of sailors. There was an air base nearby in Washington D.C. where we worked in the Navy yard. We got off the bus at the Anacostia stop. This one fellow got off with us. I said to him 'What are you going to do? Do you want to go get a cup of coffee'? He said, 'yes.' So, we made him pay for the coffee." Her best friend, Bess, has Alzheimer's disease now and doesn't remember Emily. They have been best friends and have kept in touch for over seventy years.

What was your greatest achievement in your life?

"It was being independent!"

What do you want America to know about your experiences during this time?

"They were good years for me. I made a lot of friends and did things I never would have done if I had stayed in Brooklyn. I would have married a Brooklyn boy, never done anything, worked, and had kids."

Emily and John

What did you do after the war?

Emily was discharged from the Navy on March 18, 1946. After John and Emily were married and discharged from the Navy, John did not want to move away from his family in Indianapolis. Emily moved with John, leaving her family in Brooklyn, New York. They moved in with John's mother on East Washington Street in Indianapolis. John's sister and her husband also lived in the house. Emily said, "John's mother had a big house with a large porch. We were one big happy family. We lived with John's mother for three years. Then we moved into half a double around the corner on Tacoma Street. We had two of our four kids there."

Emily worked for six months in the payroll department at Stewart Warner until her first child was born. John and Emily had four children and were married for fifty-eight years. "I said to John, 'If we ever get a divorce there will be no fight over the children; you get all of them!'" she joked.

Some years ago, Emily was part of the Navy Club for WAVES. "There were fifty members at one time, but only two are left now. Another woman and I are both in our mid-nineties. We also walked in parades for Veterans Day."

Present day ~

Vera Nuckols and Emily both went on the Indy Honor Flight on the same day. Even though they live only a few miles apart, the two veterans didn't know each other, but Emily remembered Vera's name. Both ladies say they helped pay for the Women's Memorial and felt it was well overdue in being built. Emily was disappointed that she didn't go to the Women's Memorial during her Indy Honor visit to Washington D.C. Emily said, "There is a film of pictures with the names of each person that wanted to be remembered. It was free like most things are to service people in D.C."

Georgia Brown Kamp

U.S. Army Air Corps
Patterson Field
Airplane Mechanic

Author's Note~

Each Labor Day weekend the Indiana Military Museum, Vincennes, Indiana, sponsors a program to honor WWII veterans. On September 1, 2018, Georgia attended the WWII Salute to the Military event.

Agnes Taylor Ray

Sergeant Agnes Taylor Ray, WAAC, cook
18 December 1942 - 7 July 1944
Died: 13 August 2009

"During World War Two she served with distinction in the Woman's Army Air Corps (WAAC), Eighth Air Force, in High Wycombe, England. She remained a lifelong member of the WAAC Association. She married her high school sweetheart, Clifton Ray, on February 23, 1944 while both were stationed in England." (Obituary of Agnes Taylor Ray)

Margaret "Peg" Bixler

Peg's father, a chemist, sold war bonds during WWI. "My father, Henry Koons, was a chemist at Walter Reed Army Hospital. My mother's cousin, Captain Jim Clarkson, was killed when the Japanese attacked Pearl Harbor. He was the captain of the USS *Arizona*." Peg went on to say, "My mother taught people in our neighborhood how to can vegetables. My father taught people how to start victory gardens during WWII."

How did the rationing affect you?

"The government gave me so many points. When I would go home on vacation from nursing, I would give the points to my mother to buy food. We had so many coupons for nursing shoes."

Why did you join the Cadet Nurses during WWII?

"I had always wanted to be a nurse. When I was in high school, the Cadet Nursing program became available. There were three girls in my class who became RNs. Following college, the fellas went into the service as officers or engineers. Franklin Roosevelt was the one who signed the papers for Cadet Nurse Corps classes. You had to be eighteen to sign up, and I was only seventeen, but I turned eighteen that summer, so it was okay. The government originally wanted 65,000 nurses, but they got 179,000. One hundred twenty-four thousand people finished. It was the largest group of nurses that there has ever been in military service."

Peg attended College High School. "College High School had us ahead of everyone else because of the war. The high school was connected to Montclair State Teachers College in New Jersey. You had to take an exam to get into the class. At that time there were five hundred who would take the exam; then, they would accept fifteen or sixteen for a class. The teaching students from the college sat behind us in the class. They learned from the professor who was teaching us."

What was an unexpected event that you recall?

Peg didn't graduate from nursing until June 1947, because she contracted polio while she was studying to be a nurse. "I had six months that I had to make up due to the polio. During 1945, I had to spend three months in a communicable disease hospital and three months at home. I still remember the sounds of the iron lung machines. Because I was a nurse, I had a private room. We had young nurses coming down from Bethesda Naval Hospital, and they had no idea what a mental hospital or a communicable disease hospital was. I still have people ask me, 'why did you have polio? Why didn't you have the shot?'" No one else in Peg's family developed polio; however, her younger brother and sister were quarantined for eight weeks. "I'll never live that one down." Peg said.

"I had to have so many hours of nursing. At that time, we had state mental hospitals. I was eighteen years old when I had six to eight homicidal and suicidal patients outside of Morristown, New Jersey. In 1946, we had to have three months training in a baby hospital; this training was at Columbia Presbyterian in New York. My sister ended up being my nursing supervisor. Her husband was an officer who was killed in the war. She had her BS and was teaching at a private school in Massachusetts. One day my sister came home and said, 'I am going into nursing, and I am going to Yale.' We graduated on the same day."

When she was making up her time, she worked on the maternity ward as head nurse. At this time if your husband was in the service, you could have your mother or mother-in-law be with you during labor. "I had this young woman, and it was her first baby. Her mother-in-law was with her. The baby developed heart trouble, and he was transferred over to Babies Hospital in New York City. Believe it or not, I was there when that child had his open-heart surgery, and that was very unusual then. Coming down the hall one day was this woman, and she had a military fella with her in uniform. She said, 'there is the nurse that was there when I had the baby.' And I was taking care of that baby in Babies Hospital. It was absolutely amazing."

"When you look back on it, we had a fantastic education. I didn't realize it at the time. As a cadet nurse, I was paid ten dollars a month from the Public Health Service or United States government. Our senior year we got twenty-five dollars a month. We wore the cadet nursing uniform, either summer or winter uniforms. Following polio, with time to make up, I no longer was paid, and my dad paid my nursing fees."

What was your greatest regret?

"When we signed our papers for the Cadet Nurse Corp, we had to say what branch of service we wanted to join. I signed up for the U.S. Navy. Whenever the cadet nurses graduated, they would go into the branch of service they had indicated. Due to contracting polio, I couldn't join the military. You were to serve the duration of the war. Now, I have Post-Polio Syndrome." The polio left Peg with some paralysis on the left side of her body.

Did you do any nursing after graduation?

"I didn't work because I was married. At that time, some husbands didn't believe in wives working. I did go back to school when I was forty-five and took some courses. I became an oncology nurse at a medical center in New Jersey. We were a satellite facility for Sloan-Kettering Cancer Hospital in New York City."

How did WWII affect your life?

"Well it affected everyone's life at that time. Everybody was behind it (the war). Even little kids saved tin cans that were collected and picked up once a week. We saved the foil from the cigarette packages. It is amazing how everyone was behind it (the war).

What do you do today for the military?

"I volunteer for the USO, United Service Organizations, at Reagan Airport here in Washington. People will ask us, 'what's going on?' The banners are up, and the band is playing. One day I lost it; I was pushing a young man in a wheel chair who was missing both of his legs, and someone came up to me and asked, 'What's going on?' I snapped at him, and said, 'Don't you know that wars are still going on?' I shouldn't have snapped at him. At Reagan Airport we don't have a sleeping room for babies, like Dulles Airport. It is amazing when all these guys come in. I work with a retired Air Force nurse who served overseas. The other one is the wife of a retired Air Force doctor."

During WWII the USO was staffed by volunteers who gave food and entertainment for the troops. Some famous entertainers were Bob Hope, The Andrews Sisters, Fred Astaire, and Lauren Bacall. USO volunteers would entertain and dance with soldiers at many locations around the world. Bob Hope is, perhaps, the most famous for the many trips he took to visit military personnel in WWII.

"One day, I greeted this fella when he came in, and if they are not in their uniforms, you don't know whether they are a corporal or a general. I gave him some coffee and a sandwich but didn't pay much attention to him after that. A mother came in with a four-year old, and she was crying. I went over, and said, 'Who left, grandma or daddy?' She said, 'My husband is Air Force.' I said, "My grandson is, and my brother was. So, she said, 'Where is your grandson now?' I said, 'He just returned from Liberia. He was over there for a year.' The young woman said, 'My husband is headed there now.' There were about thirty people in the room, but we weren't talking very loudly. This man turned and said to my partner, 'How does she know about Ebola in Liberia?' My partner said, 'She is a retired nurse, and her grandson served over there.'"

"I worked from twelve o'clock to six-thirty at night. I was getting ready to leave when this man came up to me and wanted to see my ID. I thought 'security is getting so wild down there. I wonder if I admitted someone that I shouldn't have.' Then at the top of his lungs he said, 'Are you Joe Bixler's grandmother?' I said, 'Yes sir, and who might you be?' The whole room stopped dead, and he turned around and said, 'Do you have a picture of your grandson in Africa getting the highest award in the country?' I said, 'Yes, I do.'" He said, 'Go look at it again. I am the general in charge of all our troops in Africa.' In the picture, he is the general who gave him the medal." The medal was given to her grandson in June 2017. This story was also written up in the USO newspaper.

What was your greatest achievement in your life?

"My greatest achievement was my family. I have two boys and two girls."

How did you and your fellow women nurses pave the way for today's women in the military or nursing?

"The military was about the same, but what bothers me is the nurses who have only two-year courses. My sister said, 'We, the three-year nurses, provide better bedside care than they do.'"

Life today...

Brigadier General Wilma Vaught, USAF, Retired, the woman responsible for the development of the Women's Memorial in Washington D.C., is Peg's Sunday School teacher. "Wilma and I are great buddies. She was in Vietnam. She is an amazing lady and goes all over the country trying to raise money. The Women's Memorial is absolutely broke. We don't get any money from the government. Don't they think that women ever did anything"?

What do you do with the Honor Flights in Virginia?

"Sixteen years ago, a group of us volunteered at Ft. Belvoir, a United States Army installation, packing boxes for the troops, food, and that kind of thing. One day someone came in and said they are going to start the honor flights up at the airport." After the honor flights started, "eleven of us went down on the tarmac, as the planes came in, we greeted them. Originally, there were seven or eight planes filled with WWII veterans seven days a week. We are lucky now if we have two planes of Korean and Vietnam veterans. Now we have over two hundred people who greet the veterans on the planes. This goes from the end of March to November."

Aileen Lasse Cloonan

Why did you join the military?

Aileen Lasse thought that someone should go into the Army since her brother, Joseph, was not able to volunteer due to his having polio as a child. She went into the service on August 4, 1945. She completed a nine-month course in physical therapy at the Cleveland Clinic and was commissioned as a second lieutenant. She had six months of academic coursework and three months of hospital practice. After that she reported to Ft. Devens, located near Boston, Massachusetts, for six weeks of basic training. "An eye-opener for me was when I went to the mess hall, and they had German prisoners of war serving and cooking the meals. I realized that Germans looked like Americans. Surprising! They were friendly and well-behaved. The food was excellent! It kept American soldiers from having to fill those slots."

What was your job?

Her first assignment was at Nichols General Hospital in Louisville, Kentucky. "There were some African-American patients on the ward, and there was a lot of hostility between African-Americans and white patients. I was on the orthopedic ward and many of the men were in traction. One patient tried to get out of bed to hit the one next to him. That was my first encounter with race problems."

She was a physical therapist on a ward of paraplegic soldiers. "There were twenty men on the ward. There were no complaints and no war stories.   The men had a rare sense of humor and camaraderie." Aileen went on to say, "A war injury is something you carry with you all your life."

Next, she was assigned to Camp Atterbury where there had been as many as 5,000 patients at one time. Since the war was ending, the government was closing down many of the facilities.   She was transferred to Letterman Hospital in San Francisco, California. She took the train from Chicago to Oakland, California, then a ferry to San Francisco. Letterman Hospital received about 2,000 American POWs, many wounded from the South Pacific.

She worked with veterans in the weight room. "These were active duty soldiers and some of them could walk and some could not. I would attach a metal frame to their shoe and then the maximum amount of weight that they could lift. They would do this many times, so the weight would improve their muscle strength.   With nerve injuries, we would use electric stimulation to make the muscles move. It seemed like magic." Aileen especially liked working with patients who had nerve injuries.

How did WWII affect your life?

"It got me out of a small town into the big city. I have had a wonderful life." Aileen went back to school at Stanford University on the GI Bill and met her future husband, Theodore, who was a WWII veteran as well. He served in the Aleutian Islands as a cryptographer. They were married twenty-nine years before he died of a heart attack.

"Before WWII, I graduated from Mt. Union College with a BS degree in Chemistry and Biology. I couldn't find a job in my field. I worked in my dad's grocery store in Alliance, Ohio, for about a year. During that time, a friend came over that I had gone to school with and she said, 'If I had your degree, I would go to the Cleveland Clinic. They are offering a physical therapy course for people to go into the Army.' I thought, I'll do that. I went to the Cleveland Clinic and interviewed with Dr. Quiring. The next thing I knew I was in a boarding house and going to school. The schooling was free, but I had to pay for my own books. I was homesick a lot."

What was an unexpected or funny event?

"In May 1948, after I received my discharge from the Army, I walked down to San Francisco Bay and tossed my uniform hat in the water." When asked why she did that, she said, "Freedom – no more discipline."

Did you find the discipline to be difficult?

"No. Since it was near the end of the war when we went into the service, we were housed in the city not on the base. We wore civilian clothes after work, and it was a normal life. We were able to travel around to other parts of California."

What was your greatest achievement in your life?

"My greatest achievement was my two daughters, Holly and Leslie. Also, I was a physical therapist for almost forty years."

What do you want America to know about your military experiences?

"The GI Bill was a godsend. Every GI should have this opportunity. My husband could not have afforded a college education without the GI Bill."

What is your greatest regret about your time in the military?

"That I didn't stay in the Army longer."

How did you and your fellow women physical therapists pave the way for today's women in WWII?

"We have learned so much about physical therapy, and what it can do. What I was doing was so simple. Now physical therapy has more treatments and technology available. Back in that day, people didn't know what physical therapy was. What I knew was that they taught children with polio to walk. So, I really didn't know about adults at that time. I saw the results of war and the repairs that can be made."

Phyllis Kickbush Craig

Phyllis, who was in the military for fourteen months, travelled to various locations around the United States as well as around the world. Phyllis enjoyed her time in the service.

What was your job or position in the military?

"I applied to the Navy and evidently didn't read the paperwork correctly. Six months later, I received a letter saying their quota was full, so I applied to the Army. My first assignment was Camp McCoy, near Tomah, Wisconsin, for basic training. From there we went to Fort Jackson in Columbia, South Carolina. V-J Day was declared while I was here. Then we went to Camp Plauche in New Orleans, Louisiana. We did not take care of any patients during this time."

"About five hundred gals shipped out on the troop transport USS *Republic*. We went through the Panama Canal, staying at Albrook Field while the ship was being repaired. Then we went to Hawaii, staying at Schofield Barracks. While there, nurses who were engaged, married, or wanted out of the service were discharged. After three weeks, we got orders to pack, as there was an inspection party coming to see why there were so many people sitting around doing nothing. I packed some clothes, some of them wet, and boarded the ship."

"We stopped in Okinawa and let some nurses off. Then we went on to Manila and docked in Manila Bay on November 11, 1946. We were not taken off the ship because it was a holiday. We sat in the hot sun that day with airplanes going over the ship and little boats going around the ship trying to see the women aboard. The next day, we were sent to the replacement depot where I got orders to go to Santo Tomas, a former university, but now a hospital with patients. After about two months, we closed the unit and went to a station hospital where we had psych and VD patients."

"I received orders for Japan. My roommate, Pat O'Leary from Chicago, and I went to the chief nurse to see if Pat could be put on the same orders. She was, and we went to the replacement depot thinking we were going to Japan. They asked for fifty volunteers for Korea. 'Where is Korea'? We volunteered and were back on a ship and docked in Inchon, Korea. There were about twenty or twenty-five soldiers who came aboard the ship that night. Pat met her future husband that night. We went to Ascom City, and I worked one day there. Then four of us gals got orders for a small hospital in Seoul, and Pat was one of the four. We four nurses became roommates in what had been an embassy house about a block from the hospital. I was there from February to August and made First Lieutenant while I was there. We came home by ship, and I was discharged at Fort Sheridan, Illinois."

What was your greatest achievement in your life?

"Becoming an RN, getting married, and having three babies. By the standards of the time, I was an old maid, twenty-six years old, by the time I got married in 1948. At least, in those days it was considered old."

How did WWII affect your life?

"I was in training at St. Theresa Hospital School of Nursing in Waukegan, Illinois, from 1940 to 1943. War was declared, but really it did not affect me because I was taken care of there. I was going to classes, studying, and taking care of patients. Then I did some nursing in Milwaukee and Chicago. In May 1945, I decided to go into the service."

What do you want America to know about your experiences?

"It has been over seventy years since I have been to Korea. Every country was interesting and how they lived. I did get to go back to Seoul, Korea after the Olympics, and it was all grown up. Today, it has golf courses and big beautiful buildings which weren't built when I was there. It was a shock to see it."

Virginia Edds Defourneaux

"When I graduated from nursing school at the end of 1943, I took a job, along with two other classmates, at Oak Ridge, Tennessee, to work for the Atomic Energy Commission. I was working there until April 1945, when I left to come back to Indiana. I was there almost two years but had no idea what was going on. It was the best kept secret the U.S. government has ever had. I worked in outpatient, and I did take care of General Groves who was in charge of the Manhattan Project." The Manhattan Project was the name for the secret work that was done on the atomic bomb. Scientists were working on this secret bomb in Oak Ridge, Tennessee, and Los Alamos, New Mexico.

"I spent my whole time there working in the Emergency Room and outpatient clinics. We did see some strange, not strange, but supposed injuries that came in from the field, but there wasn't any apparent injury. Workers came in with a code from the field, and we sent them on to decontamination. Decontamination at that time, to me, meant bacteria not radiation. We were not familiar with radiation at that time. I had no responsibility for this; they went to another area that had a decontamination chamber."

"I learned a new language while in Tennessee; we were in the south. For example, this woman came in with a boil in her armpit, and she called it a 'rizin.' We just did regular care. If someone came in with a laceration, we took care of it. We had maternity in the hospital and bed space for anything that might occur."

Why did you join the military?

"While I was working at Oak Ridge, I got word that my younger brother, Carl, had joined the military. I thought this war had been going on for quite a while, and we watched our people go off to war. It was time for me to go."

What was your job or position in the military?

"I went into the U.S. Army Nurse Corps in April 1945. I automatically was commissioned as a second lieutenant and inducted at Ft. Harrison in Indianapolis, Indiana. I did my basic training and received orders for assignment to Newton D. Baker General Hospital in West Virginia. I was only there a short time when I received orders to go overseas. By the end of July, I was on a hospital ship on the way to the Philippines. On August 6, we were out in the Pacific when the United States dropped the bomb on Japan. Then I knew what was happening at Oak Ridge, Tennessee. Everyone was jubilant onboard ship. The war was over. That was the attitude, of course, but there was still work to be done."

"I was in the Philippines for two years. My permanent assignment was on Luzon, south of Manila, at a station hospital in a small village. Our living and working conditions were very crude and hard to live and work in. All the nurses lived in buildings where the walls and roofs were made of reeds. We all slept on Army cots the entire time we were at the hospital. We stored everything in duffle bags under our cots. Our patients were housed in a tent with a gravel floor and a wooden walkway. There was only one light bulb in the whole place, and that was over the nurses' desk. So, at night we used a flashlight to take care of patients. It was a small hospital, and anything serious was sent up to the general hospital in Manila. I was in the Philippines almost two years."

Did you ever fear for your safety?

"Only one time when all us nurses were in an open-air truck, and Japanese guerillas fired on us. No, not really, just the one experience."

After WWII ended~

"After my time in the military during WWII, I was released in 1947. I returned to Dugger, Indiana, in Sullivan County. I took a job in Terre Haute, Indiana, and did private duty nursing, but I had another plan. I went back to school to get my BSN, Bachelor of Science in Nursing, to major in public health nursing. It was in 1947 when I left Indiana and went to the University of Colorado in Boulder, Colorado. I completed my work at the university in January 1952. I took a job in Denver as a visiting nurse because I needed experience in the field."

Korean War

"In January 1954, I went back into the Army for the Korean War because the recruiters were after me. I got my education, and I went back in as a captain. I was sent to Ft. Carson, Colorado, where I worked in the field of Army public health nursing. It wasn't very long before I received orders to go to Yokosuka, Japan. From there I was sent to Kyoto, Japan, for assignment. I had a scary trip to Kyoto. My ticket was for the train, late in the evening. I was new to the area and didn't know anything about the culture. I had a ticket, and somebody took me and put me on the train. I was the only Caucasian woman on the train. It was an overnight trip, but I had a sleeping berth for the night."

"The Japanese men were getting off work, and the trains were very crowded. At that time, people pushed the men through the windows. All the Japanese men started taking off their clothes and putting on their robes. They were peeling nectarines and throwing the peels in the aisles. The culture was strange to me, and I was lonely. It was a bit frightening. I was about thirty-two years old at this time. They didn't speak English, and I certainly didn't speak Japanese."

"Being a Public Health nurse, my MOS, or military occupation specialty, meant I was the only one needed here. All this was unexpected to me. It never occurred to me that I would be assigned to work totally alone. I was sent back up north to a small Army base south of Tokyo. I was the only female officer on the post. We had Marines and the Air Force and their dependents on the base. My assignment was to be responsible for the whole post without a doctor. We had two dispensaries to run. There were medics and Navy corpsmen to help. I had SOPs, standard operating procedures, which was the guide for taking care of everyone. I was responsible for the care of the school children and all the dependents as well. I had to fly out with the mothers who were pregnant to a larger hospital. You had the job, and you did it. You look back on it and wonder how you did it; and I wonder if I did a good job. We had six school teachers from the United States, and I lived with the school teachers. They were a lot of fun. I enjoyed military nursing. I had to do treatment and make diagnoses, and I was on call 24/7. However, I managed to keep my sanity."

Fukuoka, Japan

"They closed my previous post, so I was reassigned to Fukuoka, Japan. I had much the same working situation.

Again, I was the only female officer, but I did have two doctors. I lived with school teachers there also. I was here about six months, and it was getting near time for me to return to the United States. The Fukuoka post was closing, so I received orders to go to Tokyo General Army Hospital. I did work in a hospital, but I was taking care of the polio patients and soldiers in the iron lung. We had many of our men from Korea develop bulbar polio, and that is not well-known. Well, during 1955, we had the Salk vaccine, but we didn't give it to our soldiers; we gave it to our children. By the end of 1956, I received my orders to return to the United States."

What is an unexpected or funny event that you recall?

While in the Philippines, "a group of nurses were given R & R, rest and relaxation, to go to a mountain retreat called Baguio. We were transported in an open truck on dirt roads. When we reached our destination, our faces were covered in dust and dirt; it was like a dirt facial mask!   This was a really nice mountain retreat."

What is your greatest regret about your time in the military?

"I had no real regrets because it was a period of learning skills, and I enjoyed military nursing.   I finished up in the reserves and retired with twenty years of service. I used the GI Bill when I was at the University of Colorado. I worked for my room and board in the dorm."

How did WWII affect your life?

"It makes me think much more about the freedom we have in the United States. It is so wonderful to get back to your own country. You don't want to live any place else."

What do you want America to know about your experiences?

"This is the greatest country in the world. The Japanese were very nice to me. I enjoyed the Japanese people that I would meet. Meeting them on the street, especially the students, they would all carry *Readers Digest*. They would stop you on the street and say, 'may I speak English with you'? They were eager to learn English."

What was your greatest achievement in your life?

"I married Rene Defourneaux in 1965. He was retired military, and when we married, I inherited five children from his first marriage. Taking a family of five to help raise was quite a responsibility. They were ages four and one half to fourteen. Rene had a very interesting life. He worked with the French Resistance. He was born in France, but came here (United States) when he was eighteen. Then Rene went into the American Army before he was even an American citizen. He wasn't in too long before he was sent to England."

"He was trained by the British for the OSS, the Office of Strategic Services, which is special operations...the forerunner of the CIA. There were twelve or fourteen in his class, and they trained in Scotland. Out of this group, there were only about three who passed the class. It was a very rigorous course. So, he was immediately sent over to France to work with the Resistance. In 1945, he was sent to northern Vietnam to work with Ho Chi Minh because that was during the invasion of the Japanese into China."

How did you and your fellow women nurses pave the way for today's women in the military?

"There were women before us who paved the way. Of course, I don't think we nurses were responsible for paving the way because we knew what our job was. We felt comfortable because we didn't have to compete with men. Our orders came from the doctors. Nurses didn't do that much to pave the way for women in general. Other women paved the way for us. I retired with the rank of major."

Norma Defino Nelson

"My Italian father came to this country when he was seventeen and settled in Chicago. I think they had to learn English then. He married my mother, and they had three girls - two became nurses and one a teacher. He had a restaurant during this time."

Do you remember when the war began?

"I had graduated from high school and was in a small Christian college in Missouri on December 7, 1941. We got up the next morning; all the fellows had gone to enlist. At the semester, I went home to enroll in nurse's training instead of being a teacher. When the war started there were very few Army nurses; there wasn't any need for them. So, many women became nurses after the war started. Our country was attacked, so everybody wanted to do something for the war: victory gardens, or something."

How did WWII affect your life?

"I was in Wisconsin for basic training; then, the Army shipped us down to Charleston, South Carolina, and we ended up boarding the ship there."

Why did you join the military?

"In 1942, I joined the Army because the war started, and I was discharged in January 1947, from Camp Kilmer, New Jersey. Also, I stayed in the reserves for a while. There were twelve of us that graduated from the three-year nursing program and went into the service. My sister was a nurse in the Philippines, and fortunately, she came home safely."

What was your job or position?

U.S. Army Hospital Ship, *Shamrock*

"I was in the Army Nurse Corps. In 1945, the war had ended, but we were still sent overseas. We were headed to the Pacific where they put three hundred nurses on a broken-down ship, U.S. Army Hospital Ship *Shamrock*, for a month. There was a typhoon that hit Okinawa and had damaged the ship. It was sunk at Anzio during a battle there. They brought it back to Charleston, North Carolina, for repair. On the voyage, we broke down before we got to Panama, and we broke down after we got to Panama."

"They would not allow us to go onto the deck. We waited on Gatun Lake for five days." According to www.med-dept.com, the USAHS *Shamrock*, originally the USAT *Agwileon*, capsized in port in 1941. After the ship was repaired, it was renamed the USAHS *Shamrock* and converted to a hospital ship. The ship was scrapped in February 1948.

"We tossed and turned while in the Pacific, as it was really rough. We really didn't think we were going to make it. We had to wear life jackets all the time. There were more cockroaches on the ship than people. You had to shake out the life jacket before you put it on to make sure there were no bugs in it. Finally, the ship pulled into a Mexican port, and the executive decision was made that we couldn't get across the Pacific in that ship. Our foot lockers were down below in the hold and were getting wet, so they took us off the ship in Los Angeles."

"The ship was dismantled, and the nurses were sent cross country to various posts. I was sent to Camp Kilmer, New Jersey. The captain was court-martialed for inappropriate conduct toward the women soldiers, and the dentist was court-martialed because he was a drunk and pulled the wrong teeth."

"The kids were coming back from the European theater, and I saw more things than I had ever seen before in a regular hospital – more wounds and amputations. They were shipping the soldiers to Camp Kilmer and to general hospitals near their families. After things calmed down a little bit, the military was sending war brides back. You could sign up to accompany them to Chicago on the train. It was interesting, as they wanted so many nurses on those trains. I made two trips to Chicago with the war brides."

What do you remember about the end of the war?

"Oh my, it was wild. We were in Charleston, South Carolina, waiting to go aboard ship. No horns were allowed in this area. All of a sudden, the whole place went crazy; horns were honking...the war had ended. Are we still going to go overseas? Yes, we are going to go overseas. So, we did."

What is an unexpected or funny thing that happened during this time?

"There was an American Indian WAC who had a baby during this time. I was working on the Obstetrics floor. She tried to deliver the baby by herself, which didn't work out. He was named Chiefie and a darling little boy. The nurses had him for two years. He wasn't adopted and went through the foster system."

After the war~

"I went to work at Wesley Hospital in Chicago on the Psych Ward for five years. Then, I did private duty nursing and married in 1953. I met my husband, Russell Nelson, in a hospital, and I didn't work again. He lived in Chicago, and he and all the young men on his street, and in his area, marched down to volunteer. The doctor in charge examined Russell and said, 'Go home fella, you aren't going to live long enough to see the war.' Ironically, Russell lived to be ninety-five years old."

What was your greatest achievement in your life?

"Learning to be a nurse and doing the things that I did. I think I have used my nursing training, and I am still doing it. I am a Type-A personality, and I find people to help all the time."

How did you and your fellow women soldiers pave the way for today's women in the military?

"I think it increased the number of women in the military. It gave them rank that they never had before."

What do you want America to know about your experiences in the military?

"That everybody wanted to do something when we were attacked. It was entirely different than the Vietnam War. The sharpest young men from my class of 1942 took Air Force training, and they were killed. They took the youngest and brightest. It was interesting that I met a woman in the service whose husband had been killed. She waited until after they had emptied all the prison camps to be sure that her husband, Jim, was not alive. Then she joined the Army. It was a time that everybody wanted to do something."

Do you have any regrets about your time in the military?

"I don't have any regrets. Being in New York and being in uniform, New York treated us very well. We got to go to plays and things in New York City."

"In 2014, I took the Indy Honor Flight to Washington D.C. I met Bob and Elizabeth Dole while we were there. He said, 'What did you do in the war, young lady?' I said, "I was a nurse." He said, 'I wouldn't be alive if it weren't for you women.' Also, when we visited Arlington National Cemetery, I laid the wreath on the tomb of the unknown soldier. I told the soldier there that he had made the daughter of an Italian immigrant very happy. When we came home from the service, we didn't get the kind of thanks that we get now."

Marion "Nan" Somes

Marion "Nan" Somes served in the overseas area of Anzio Beach, Italy and North Africa. She also spent some time in Paris, France when she was on leave.

What was your job or position?

Marion Nancy Malik lived in Elyria, Ohio, and graduated from

high school in 1935. She did her nursing training at M.B. Johnson School of Nursing in Elyria, Ohio and graduated in 1939. Nan went into military service on June 1, 1942, as a reserve nurse in the Army Nurse Corps. She was sent to La Garde General Hospital, New Orleans, Louisiana. "This was a port of debarkation for the troops. There were fifteen of us that helped get the hospital started."

"The nurses followed the troops in the war. When the troops received their orders to go into the war zone, the nurses would follow shortly thereafter to establish hospitals in the war zone."

Why did you join the military?

"They needed nurses during the war because there were lots of fatalities. I wanted to do my part and be available to take care of the wounded."

What did your family think of your joining the military?

"My father, Joseph, and my mother, Frances immigrated from Czechoslovakia prior to the war. My dad was always connected to the Army and was proud that I was joining the military. After my parents left Czechoslovakia, they never returned."

What was an unusual event?

Tony Minutillo, a medical corpsman, drew several pencil drawings depicting many events that took place during her time in Italy. This is an example of one of his drawings.

"I never saw Tony after the war, as he came from New York. He used to call me Sarge," said Nan.

Describe what happened at Anzio Beach, Italy?

"I had only been there a couple days when the head nurse came to me in the hospital tent where I was working and told me to go right now with this corpsman. Tell him where your tent is, and he will dig a foxhole for you. So, I went with him, and the head nurse stayed with my patient while I was gone. He didn't get two shovels dug when he said, 'Jump into any of the foxholes you see here.' I jumped down, and there was water in it. There was a horrible bomb explosion. When we got out of the foxhole, I followed him back to the tent that I had just left. There were sixty-five men and the woman that I was taking care of in the tent, plus the nurse that was covering for me."

"When I returned there was nothing left of the long tent. The nurse who took over for me was dead, and so was the patient that I was nursing. All the men were killed as well. It is an experience I will never forget." Nan talked her fellow nurse, Mary, into going up to Anzio with her. "Mary was not hurt in the bombing that killed the others in the tent. Mary was in a different tent during the bombing."

Nan has shrapnel pieces that exploded near her during another attack. "When shrapnel comes down, it is red hot and the edges are sharp, and It just cuts people. When you are getting bombed, and it hits the ground it comes apart." It just missed Nan. She didn't remember the exact details of this event with the shrapnel.

Nan met Ernie Pyle briefly while he was on Anzio Beach. She said she had a chance to talk to him, while he was checking on the troops who were injured. "He came up to the tent to visit the men."

"As a reward for volunteering for Anzio Beachhead, they (the military) gave us a present. They let us go to Paris and do whatever we wanted to do. I wanted to go to the hairdresser. This was when they had these great big hairdos." Nan and some of the other nurses enjoyed some time away in France.

Describe your time in North Africa

"I was assigned to the 21st General Hospital in North Africa. That hospital originated from St. Louis. We docked at Oran and went south to Vou Hanifia where we had a hospital. We didn't stay there long because the troops were moving north across the Mediterranean to Italy. We followed them, and we went to Naples where the wounded were being brought to be cared for."

GRANDE HOTEL — BOU-HANIFIA — NORTH AFRICA

"When we were transported from one place to another, we rode in trucks. My husband, John, saw me jumping down from a truck in Oran, North Africa. It's a port city on the coast of North Africa. We were talking and got to know each other when we were in Italy. We later married."

Letters from home~

Letters from home were the highlight of a soldier's life during combat. Nan has saved some letters from her parents. The letters are written in bohemian or Czech, but Nan could read some of the words. The gist of the letter from her dad talked about Nan's losing a tooth. "He was wishing me a happy new year and good health." Nan's dad wrote, "I am healthy, but I have a big thirst all the time."

"The family lived in a multi-lingual neighborhood in Elyria, Ohio. These families had moved to America from Europe and still spoke their native language – Greek, Slovak, Czech, Polish, German. My father was called the 'Mayor' of this community of immigrants – it was called Honkeyville. Any time you needed someone to go to court with you, my dad would put on his derby hat and go with them. People would say, 'Call Joe Malik, he will go with you.' People respected him."

What was your greatest achievement in your life?

"To become an Army nurse, and to do the things I was able to do (for the war.)" She received several certificates of commendation for her service during the war.

How did WWII affect your life?

"I was very thankful I was able to be a nurse and be of help to those that needed it. I met my husband, John, and was married. We had two sons that have passed away. Also, my brother Frank, a mechanical engineer, was killed on Luzon, Philippines, during WWII."

What is your greatest regret about your time in the military?

"I am blessed that I was able to be there. I was so attached to so many of the soldiers and lost so many of them."

Drawing by Tony Minutillo

Author's note~

On April 27, 2018, Nan died after spending over 101 years on Earth helping others. She was laid to rest with full military honors on Sunday, May 20, 2018, on a beautiful, sunny day. She would have been pleased with the send-off.

Juliette "Julie" Thomas

Julie was able to wear her WWII Army uniform after more than seventy years. She is a proud veteran who was committed to helping injured soldiers during her time in the military.

How did WWII affect your life?

"Well, at that time, I was a young girl in my twenties, and it was quite an experience. I wasn't glad to have the war to have that experience. Also, I liked the small-town nursing experience where you have pregnant ladies, accidents, and everything coming in. It was good for my nursing experience."

Why did you join the military?

"I joined the military because, at the time, there was a world war. Our young people were going overseas to die. I graduated from the University of Michigan School of Nursing in Ann Arbor, Michigan. It really meant a lot to me to look back at the many people I had graduated with and were already in the war fighting. I thought I should do my duty. The day that the war ended everybody was delighted. The newspapers were filled with stories with good feelings in them. Everybody was celebrating because the Germans had finally surrendered. When the Japanese surrendered, it was a very happy time for the United States too."

What was your job or position?

"First of all, with my induction into the Army Nurse Corp as an Army nurse, I was sent to Camp McCoy, Wisconsin. When I was taken into the Army, we were sent to an Army camp. In New Jersey, we boarded a huge gray troop ship on our way to England. It had been an ocean liner and was a beautiful ship. We sailed at 2 a.m. across the ocean from the New Jersey dock. Before we sailed, our leaders had us climb a steep river bank. I don't know why, but it was covered with poison ivy. I was severely allergic to poison ivy. Sure enough, three days after we were at sea, I broke out with poison ivy. I recovered down in the sickbay. We had to zigzag across the ocean because there were reports of an enemy submarine in the area. Every time we had to zigzag it was hard to walk down the hallway."

"Because it was a British ship, the British didn't know anything about poison ivy. The poison ivy blisters were extremely painful. What I had to do was open the door to the cabin to let in the cool air. This helped my poison ivy feel better. Before I knew it, the captain of the ship and the head of our troop contingent appeared at my bedside. They said I was trying to seduce the ship steward who was walking by my room at night. It was only the cool air that I was trying to find. I told the captain and the head of our contingent, 'If you will let me have a cabin with a bathtub in it, since you don't know what to do for poison ivy, and a box of baking soda, I'll take care of it.' I spent the rest of that voyage across the Atlantic Ocean in a tub of cool water. It finally worked."

"When we arrived in Europe, our ship was diverted to the harbor in Edinburgh. There was an enemy submarine that was after us. We did finally get there, thank goodness."

"That's where I recovered in the U.S. Army hospital in Edinburgh, Scotland. That was quite a wonderful entry into Army life. When I was fully recovered, I was sent by train from Edinburgh to the southern coast of England. It was remarkable to see all the towns that had been bombed. I was allowed to get off the train when it stopped and look around. In some places, there was only a chimney standing where the Germans had blasted the area. When we arrived in London, there was one part of the famous church, St. Paul's Cathedral, that had been blown out. That really impressed me."

"Anyway, I did get down to where they sent me just outside of town in an Army hospital. It looked like the gates into a MASH television program. It was composed of stone and cement blocks with tin roofs, and each unit had a tent alongside it. Each unit had thirty patients, so we would have ninety patients in all. We had three corpsmen to help us, and that is how I spent the war."

"The injured were brought over at midnight by the troops from France because that was where the main fighting was at that time. The men had been attended to by the unit in back of the fighting on the front lines. That's how they did it then; you had the front lines and the surgical unit in back, then, these lesser units which is where I was sent. The medical staff tried to heal their wounds, so soldiers could be sent back into battle. I was really discouraged with the Army because sometimes the men came back three times."

"The men had to go back into battle; otherwise, they were sent back to the United States if they weren't able to go back into battle. I thought it was terrible they would be sent back into battle three times. The injured soldiers had done their duty. I did enjoy my Army career and my small-town office career. I enjoyed it all until we went back into civilian life."

"After the war ended in Europe, the nurses were on the first boat sent back, and we were to go to the Pacific war or Japanese war. The military gave us a nice furlough, and my girlfriend and I went down to St. Ives. My husband-to-be, George, met me at the Chicago railroad station. The military didn't carry troops by plane, but by rail. The loudspeaker came on saying, 'Will Lieutenant Hone please leave your car and come to the station. There is an important person waiting to greet you.' Our head nurse was in our train car, and she said to everyone, 'Go look out there and see what happens.' My fiancé, George, had borrowed the commander's limousine, and that was how I came into this country. He had already set up the wedding with the church ladies in the town where I lived. Everything was planned, and I couldn't believe it. We were married and had a little honeymoon."

"After we were married, I stayed in the Army. We were going to Fort Lewis, Washington, and then to the Pacific where the Allies were fighting the Japanese. However, before we were shipped out, the Japanese surrendered. They sent me to a hospital in a small town in North Dakota instead. I got a taste of the small-town nursing. I was in the Army about two years and didn't go any further because my husband insisted that I leave the military. I would have loved to go on further. He was an Army captain, so I did as I was told."

"After I left the military, I served in a hospital town as a night nurse. I worked as a physician's nurse in a small town. The doctor was the most popular physician in town, and it was a lot of fun."

"When the war ended, my husband decided we would move to the San Francisco Bay area. I got a job in one of the city hospitals. Finally, he wanted me to not work anymore. So, it was a very short nursing career actually."

What is your greatest regret about your time in the military?

"Never, never. Even when I was at the University of Michigan, I knew what I needed to do. So many people I had graduated with from high school were already in it or killed."

What do you want America to know about your experiences?

"I just want to say everyone is different and everyone has a different idea about their feelings. My feelings were that I owed it to my country and my friends that had already gone into war, and I wanted to do my duty. It gave me a feeling that I had accomplished something."

What was your greatest achievement in your life?

"I think it was raising my family. I have four boys."

What was an unexpected experience during this time?

"My family was involved in 4-H during this time. We had these big steers, and you had to be very careful. The steers have a problem with their alimentary canal or something because they will bloat. So, I taught my eldest son what to do when this happened. You cannot let them lie down because you can't get them back up. That's when I ran and got the plastic garden hose. I got the Vaseline out and told my son to hold that big head up because it was going down. Then I put the hose in, and we saved that lovely big steer. My nursing training helped, but that's what we do. Nurses are told what the duty is, and we do it."

How did you and your fellow women nurses pave the way for today's women in the military?

"Well, I hope nurses are given a history of what went on before. I know that nurses are given much more authority than we were. The main thing is to do your duty and your job as well as you can. It gives you a good feeling to know that you have done your job."

Alberta Stanley White

In February 1923, five-year old Alberta and her family left Albany, Georgia and moved to Indianapolis, Indiana. There were eight children in the family. When the family arrived by train, there was snow on the ground. In 1937, she graduated from Crispus Attucks High School.

How did WWII affect your life?

"It opened doors that I would not have gotten in without having been a veteran. After the war, I worked at the Finance Center at Fort Harrison in Indianapolis. Then, I was a practical nurse when I worked in the VA Hospital which is what I wanted to do before the war. I worked there for five or six years. I was helping a patient get back into his bed when we both fell. The fall hurt my back, and I had to leave the hospital. Then I returned to the Finance Center to work. It opened doors for a lot of people."

What was your job or position in the military?"

"I joined the Army and was a medical technician and administrative clerk. It was on the job training. The WACs wore a uniform like a nurse's aide. When we were in class, if a patient came in and we were studying that particular subject, we had to go over and watch the procedure. We didn't have to go to our book to find out how to do it; we saw it. We learned how to put bandages on. We already knew how to take temperatures and blood-pressure. We didn't draw blood, but we could hang blood and IVs. The practical nurses were the ones that did more. We did more in the military than nurses would do as a civilian. Being a practical nurse, we didn't do half of the things we did in the service."

"I had taken some classes at the Red Cross before I went into the service. The Red Cross taught a class on being a nurse's aide which was required to get into the WACs. That's why we didn't have to go through the training."

"I did my basic training in Des Moines, Iowa. The military divided the group up with one group going to Michigan, and the other going to Chicago. Since Chicago was closer to home, I hoped I could be stationed in Chicago. The military tended to send you where you didn't want to go. So, I was like a fox by saying to everyone, 'I hope you send me to Michigan.' I was later stationed at Gardiner General Hospital in Chicago, Illinois. I stayed a year and a half in the regular Army and some of the time in the reserves. When I was at the Finance Center in Indianapolis, I was called back for active duty. When you joined the WACS, it was as a volunteer for three years."

"Every time I got a chance, I was on that train to Indianapolis. I would be late getting back to camp and my superior, Lieutenant Brown, would say, 'And don't be coming in telling me about my brother at Attucks.' Lieutenant Brown's brother was the music teacher at Attucks High School where I had attended high school. She would say, 'Get that bucket and start washing those windows.' I washed a lot of windows and picked up a lot of trash because I would always be late getting back. I would be sitting talking with my family and miss the train back. I was honorably discharged from Gardiner General Hospital in Chicago, Illinois."

Why did you join the military?

"I joined the military because I wanted to work in the government hospital, and the administration wouldn't hire me. I wanted to be a cadet nurse, but my grades were not good enough for me to get into the program. So, they told me to try to join the WACs. To work in the government hospital, I had to join the WACS. So, I had to be a WAC, which wasn't my idea at all. It was okay, not something I loved, but it was a job. The pay was so much better than anything that I had been doing in civilian life. Also, the benefits were good, and I could send my mother a check every time I got paid. I was five-foot three inches tall and weighed one hundred and three pounds. I have always been small. When I went to join the service, I got on the scales, but couldn't pass the weight requirement. You had to weigh a hundred pounds to join. So, they took me in another room and fed me bananas, and I drank water. Then I got on the scales again; the scales got to one hundred pounds."

"When I was marching to breakfast, the Military Police would come around and put rocks in my pockets to keep me from blowing away. When I was issued my uniform, it always had to be sent to the seamstress because I was so little. I was the smallest one in my class and the smallest in my family. My mother used to call me 'little gal' when I was growing up."

After the war ~

"I met my husband, Overton, on a blind date in 1946. I was still in uniform, and my girlfriend fixed me up with a blind date. He had just gotten out of the service and had money to spend. He showed me a good time. Count Basie was in town and Overton had a table reserved. Count Basie was playing at the Sunset Terrace on Indiana Avenue in Indianapolis. We were sitting in front of the band. Overton was buying everybody drinks, and when we were introduced he said, 'hi, Baby.' I have been known as 'Baby' ever since. When I went back to the service, he would send me magazines and chocolates. I love to dance, and Overton could dance."

During the 1930's and 1940's, all the big bands came to Indianapolis. It was a popular night spot on 'The Avenue.' Some notable big bands and singers were Jimmy Lunsford, Wes Montgomery, and Count Basie. The historic Madame Walker Theatre is also located in this same area.

"Overton's grandmother was an Irish war bride, and he spent a lot of time with his grandparents. So, he grew up around many white children. Overton attended Manual High School because they were a mixed-race family. When Attucks High School was built just for blacks, he refused to go to Attucks. He dropped out of school and finished his education in night school." In May 1953, Alberta and Overton married when she was thirty-five, and he was forty-three. They didn't have any children.

"There was a group of veterans who were friends after the war. There were three guys, and I was the only girl. The Army was still paying us until we got a job. So, we would go different places to apply for jobs. Overton was my best friend, and I fell in love with my best friend. Overton died in June 1980."

Did you have any regrets from your time in the military?

"None, what so ever. I don't have any regrets."

What was your greatest achievement in your life?

"I haven't done anything outstanding. When my pastor was talking about me at my one hundredth birthday party, I had to look around to see who he was talking about."

What do you want America to know about your experiences?

"I was raised in a Christian family, and I give credit to my Lord Jesus Christ who got me through some difficult times. Trust in the Lord with all your heart. He has led me, and I am still leaning on Him."

How did you and your fellow women soldiers pave the way for today's women?

"We learned how to stick to the rules; when the Army said, 'to do it this way,' we did it this way. We were marching, and everyone loved to dance. We would be marching, and the lieutenant would say, 'Don't you go jitterbugging around the corner either.' All the world is watching you, so we have to do everything right."

Brigadier General Wilma L. Vaught, USAF, Retired

General Wilma L. Vaught was the first woman in history to deploy with an Air Force bomber wing; one of the early women to reach the rank of brigadier general and the first in the comptroller field. She retired in 1985 from the military.

Women's Memorial

"It was not my idea to build a memorial to women in the military. I had never given it any thought ever. I retired to the Washington D.C. area, and there were about five of us who were women generals or admirals who were retired and could serve on the board of directors for the Memorial foundation. The others were not interested in doing it, so I told them I would serve on the board, but I would not agree to be president. In 1987, I missed a meeting and got a phone call from one of the members asking why I wasn't at the meeting. I said, 'what meeting? I forgot all about it. I didn't go. What did you do?' She said, 'We elected new officers, and you are the new president.'"

"I had to give a lot of thought about my feelings about a memorial for military women, because as military members, we had worked hard to integrate with men. We had made a lot of progress. There were those who felt if we built a memorial dedicated to the women, this could separate us again from that close association. I was one that felt that way; that perhaps we shouldn't do this - to set ourselves apart. Then I began to travel around the country and talk about building a memorial. It became evident to me that this was a very important issue, particularly for women who served in WWII. There were a few women who had served in WWI, and they were very interested in it, too. But, it was a major issue with WWII women because they listened to the rhetoric about the Vietnam Memorial - where nobody said thanks or paid tribute to the Vietnam veterans. The WWII women said, 'what about us? We haven't been recognized either.'"

"Some women had dedicated a small women's monument in Ohio and invited Congresswoman Mary Rose Oakar, a congresswoman from Toledo, to speak. The women asked her, 'what about us?' Congresswoman Oakar said, 'what do you mean you haven't been recognized? You are part of all these memorials.' The women said, 'no, we are not.' She had her staff check, and they found that the memorials were basically a tribute to the men. They were not a tribute to both men and women. So, it was Congresswoman Mary Rose Oakar who got the legislation passed for the Memorial to be built in Washington D.C. or its environs."

"The more I talked to women, the more I became convinced that this was something we had to do, and this probably would be the only opportunity we would have to do it. If we were going to do it, we had to do it right. We couldn't just throw something up and say, 'this is it'. We had to think it through and do it right. One woman on the board of directors, Helen Jeffrey, who had served as a TECH3 WAC in WWII, volunteered to work with me. We concluded what we ought to do, as opposed to creating a statue or some type of monument, was to tell the story of women's service because no one had been collecting the pieces of paper or anything else that were related to the history of military women. We needed to tell the history of women's service...what they did, where they served, how they felt about it and pay tribute to them. Therefore, we needed a structure."

"Among the many sites shown to us by the National Park Service was this site at the entrance to Arlington National Cemetery. Here, we felt we had space to build. It was on the tourist path, and there was a relationship between that site and women's service. We talked to the people at the Park Service, and they said it would cost between four and six million dollars to take care of the deterioration of the site that had taken place during the last thirty years. After much thought by both us and the Park Service, we all agreed it was the ideal location for the Women's Memorial. The site was approved by the required federal agencies to be the location for the Memorial."

Donations

"We wrote letters and asked for donations. We had a design competition, and we had more than one hundred and thirty-two submissions. We had highly qualified individuals serve as judges who selected the winning design and we proceeded on, although some adjustments to the original design had to be made. At one time, we thought the Memorial would be underground. But the winning design had the Education Center behind the existing hemicycle wall. So, the hemicycle wall actually forms one wall of the Education Center."

"The major issue was getting the money to proceed. It was extremely difficult, but we didn't give up. This was our only opportunity, so we had to do something, and we had to do it right. We will get it done. We decided not to include any statues because of the evolution of roles, ranks, and uniforms of women over the years. We didn't think that a statue should be any part of it – how could you ever capture the changes in a statue?"

"When we first started collecting money, we would get checks in the mail and boxes of uniforms, shoes, and medals that women, or their families, had been saving all these years, and they wanted them to be part of the Memorial. So, we started collecting things that we could have in the various exhibits."

Funding for the Memorial now

"We went to all the states in the country and got every state to donate money in honor of their women veterans. Each one donated except the District of Columbia. This was a one-time contribution to the Memorial from the states. We have talked, however, about going back to the states again. One thing I have learned is, it is easier to get money to build than money to operate. The problem now is a lack of operating funds. When I was newly retired, I knew a lot of generals who had retired and were at corporations. So, I told Helen, one of the only things going for us is that I am a retired general, 'I am not going to be Wilma, I am going to be General Vaught.' So that's what I have been all the way through – General Vaught. Generally speaking, people who have known me for twenty years call me, General."

"One year we were able to get a donation of five million dollars from Congress. It came at a wonderful time. Juanita Millender-McDonald, a California Congress- woman, was a supporter of the Women's Memorial. She was chairman of the Congressional Woman's Caucus at that time. She set up a committee to place a wreath at the Women's Memorial for Memorial Day. I had gone to see her when I needed five hundred thousand dollars for the Memorial. Congresswoman Millender-McDonald went to see Congressman Jack Murtha from Pennsylvania and we got five hundred thousand dollars. She said that next year she would get us a million dollars. For the next three years, she was able to get us a million dollars each year. Then she developed cancer and died. I went to her funeral because she believed in us. She felt that the women in Congress would support her. They still come and bring roses. We save the rose petals and use them during our Memorial Day program to pay tribute to military women who died or were killed in action during the past year or a woman veteran who had died. The rose petals are placed in the pool in their memory. It is a tradition we started at the Memorial's dedication and continue today."

Photo courtesy: Women in Military Service For America Memorial Foundation. Photo by Carol Highsmith

Where do you see the future of the Women's Memorial?

"I think the future of the Memorial, in some ways, remains to be seen because it is going to have to be picked up and supported by the people that just recently got out of the service or are serving today. This Memorial was basically built because of the WWII women. They were at a time in their life where they were looking back at what they did in WWII. Their service had become far more important to them, than when they got out of the service at the end of the war. It became important to them that their children and grandchildren and future generations know that they served their country in WWII. They loved this country, and they served to preserve it. It is a tremendous feeling when I meet one of the Honor Flights. When the Honor Flight women come into the Memorial and see their picture and story, the tears flow. We had one woman, Lucy Coffey, a WWII WAC staff sergeant, who came when she was 108 years old; and another one, Emma Didlake, a WWII WAC private, who was 110 years old. They wanted to see their Memorial before they died. The Honor Flights also arranged for them to visit the President and Vice-President as well as see the WWII Memorial."

USO – Service Clubs in the United States

Throughout the United States many USO, United Service Organizations, have provided an opportunity to find a friendly face and refreshments for lonely servicemen. The USO, founded February 1941, was a way that some young ladies could do something for the war effort. They are a nonprofit organization that provided programs such as comedians and musicians to the members of the military.

Stuart, Florida

In 1942, one such USO organization, Service Men's Canteen, was established in Stuart, Florida. A permanent building was built, renamed, Stuart Civic Center, and dedicated in 1943. According to the tcpalm website, "The Martin County Servicemen's Club officially opened October 1943 on Flagler Avenue. It provided a permanent rec center for troops stationed at Camp Murphy, Jensen Coast Guard Station and Fort Pierce Port with dancing, ping-pong, reading, and card rooms, creating an opportunity for the enlisted men to mingle with local citizens, including the many single young ladies in town."

Evansville, Indiana

As was the common practice with USO centers, this one was closed after the end of WWII. It was located on 8th Street near downtown Evansville. Evansville, Indiana, is adjacent to the Ohio River that divides Indiana and Kentucky. Many of the soldiers from Fort Breckinridge came to Evansville to visit the USO center. There were dances at the USO downtown and at Fort Breckinridge. There were soldiers everywhere in Evansville and Indianapolis. The building has been torn down, but the pillars from the front of the building were made into a memorial to soldiers.

USO – Today

The USO is still active today and provides comfort to traveling military personnel and their families in many airports in the United States. The USO lounges, staffed by volunteers, include various amenities and comfortable seating for servicemen and servicewomen. They want to honor veterans and active duty personnel for the service to the country.

ROSIE THE RIVETERS

As many healthy American men were being inducted into the military, women filled the vacancies left by their departure. The poster and familiar image of the working woman was Rosie the Riveter. Women who worked in war related factories during 1941 to 1945 were called "Rosies." The riveter refers to the fact that many of the women worked assembling airplane parts which were held together by rivets. There were a large number of Rosies who worked in the aircraft industry; there were also women workers making uniforms, ammunition, and other war items.

Was there a real Rosie the Riveter?

According to the website of the American National Biography, "Rose Will Monroe and Rose Bonavita, iconic figure of the women who worked in defense industries during World War II, was a composite of the experiences of many real women." However, *The New York Times* reported in January 2018, after Naomi Parker Faley's death at age 96, "the real Rosie the Riveter was a California waitress named Naomi Parker Fraley. Mrs. Fraley had worked in a Navy machine shop during World War II. It also ruled out the best-known incumbent, Geraldine Hoff Doyle, a Michigan woman whose innocent assertion that she was Rosie was long accepted." There seems to be a difference of opinion of the true identity of Rosie.

Why was the Rosie the Riveter founded?

There are many Rosies who worked in defense plants around the United States. The American Rosie the Riveter Association states, "American Rosie the Riveter Association was founded to honor working women of World War II and to recognize and preserve the history and legacy of working women." Additionally, daughters of Rosies are referred to as Rosebuds.

There are groups of present day Rosies who keep the history alive by gathering together at conventions and presentations at veterans' programs. One such person is Angie Timan whose grandmother was a Rosie. Angie is an Indiana school teacher who dresses the Rosie part, collects artifacts of this time period, and teaches history in a very real way.

Why do we need a Rosie the Riveter Association?

In 1941-1945, many women no longer stayed home and took care of the children. It was time for women to contribute to the war effort in one of the ways which they could be helpful: join the work force. Up until this time, factory work was primarily done by men. It is important for history to record this critical time in history for women's contributions.

Mildred, a Rosie from World War II, and Angie Timan.

Rosie the Riveter Memorial

The Rosie the Riveter Memorial, Richmond, California in Marina Bay Park was established in 2000. According to the National Park Service website, during World War II six million women entered the workforce. "Rosie the Riveter and her 'We can Do It' motto came to symbolize all women Home Front workers." Women starting to go to work and not wanting to leave small children at home led to the development of child care centers.

Kaiser Shipyards, located in the Richmond, California, area built 747 ships during WWII. The SS *Red Oak Victory* is the last remaining victory ship built in the Richmond Shipyards.

Bertha "Bert" Baker

How did WWII affect your life?

"It made me get up early...I didn't want to. It made life better because I had money in my pocket. I was making so much money; I didn't have any idea what a dollar meant because I was the youngest in the family. I just assumed everybody had that. My father worked for the railroad, so he worked all during the Depression and during the war. I bought a lot of war bonds and saved them. At a later time, I cashed them in and thought I was rich."

What did you and your family do for the war effort?

"I worked at Servel, Whirlpool, and the Shipyards in Evansville, Indiana. Servel built airplane wings for the P-47 Thunderbolt fighter plane. Whirlpool built washing machines prior to WWII. When the war started, they began producing components for the P-40 Warhawk aircrafts and military equipment. I was a riveter and had to go to riveting school. I didn't pass the small riveter test, but I was on a riveter that two women were needed to do the job. We worked on the ammunition boxes and on the P-47s. I put the rivet in, and I would hold the ammunition box together. Then, the bigger girl behind me would squeeze the gun and put the rivet into the metal."

"If it didn't go in straight, the inspector would not accept it. Then I would be the one to drill it out. It was interesting because on the drill that took the rivet out was on a swivel, and I would go in the middle of it and punch it out. When we would get it right, it had to be inspected again."

"My sister, June, also worked at Servel. She was my ride to work, but we didn't work together. I didn't like to get up early. We got up before daylight and were on the job. The money was good, and I worked at Servel for about a year. I changed my birth certificate, so that I could get a job at the plant. I was fifteen at the time, and you had to be sixteen to work there."

"I remember they had no need for rivets at one time, so I sat down at a big table with other women and sorted rivets. We sorted rivets by size."

Evansville Shipyards – "I rode a bicycle around to the different huts where I would take blueprints. One day it was rainy, and the railroad tracks were wet. I fell down and knocked myself out momentarily. I haven't been on a bike since then. I quit working at the shipyards soon after that. When I rode the bike around the shipyards, the guys would whistle and carry on. I would get so embarrassed. I didn't like that, so I quit that job."

Dancing with soldiers~

"My sister, June, and I rode a bus over to Camp Breckinridge, Kentucky and danced with the soldiers. It was so much fun. This one fella danced and threw me out and made my skirt come up." Camp Breckinridge, near Morganfield, Kentucky, held thousands of soldiers and German Prisoners of War. The camp was disbanded in 1949.

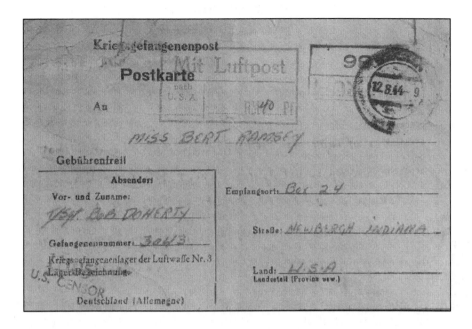

As part of the war effort, Bert also wrote letters to soldiers. One particular soldier, Bob Doherty, wrote letters back to Bert. Also, Bob was a prisoner of war in Germany and sent a "postkarte" from his time in the POW camp. Bert lost contact with Bob and wondered what happened to him after all these years.

"I met Bob one time when my sister and I were at Camp Breckinridge. In one letter he tells of his friend who took off in a plane, crashed, and died. Bob had to identify his friend's body."

What do you remember when the war began?

"I remember it vividly because my mother was so upset that my brother would have to go into the service. My brother, James, joined the Navy. Mom listened to the radio for the war news."

What do you want America to know about your experiences during WWII?

"I want America to know that we will always have to fight for our liberties, even though there are those who say we don't want to fight. I don't want fighting or war either, but when our country was freed from the English – we had to fight. We have had to fight continuously since then for one reason or another. I think we will have another war before too long."

What was your greatest achievement?

"I met John before the war. He was not in the service because of poor eyesight." John and Bert were married December 1, 1945. "I was eighteen years old when we were married. Our first child was born in November 1946." John and Bert went on to have thirteen children, or as Bert teased – a Baker's Dozen. "My greatest achievement was having all those children. It wasn't my most fun thing. Singing and dancing was what I enjoyed the most which I got into when the children were in high school."

Vi Barlow

How did WWII affect your life?

"I remember the rationing, and you couldn't get certain items. Mainly, we would dry out the coffee grounds and reuse them again." Foods like sugar, flour, and coffee were limited and people had to use ration coupons. "We learned to make do with what we had."

Do you remember the beginning of the war?

"Yes, we were in shock. I guess that's the word that comes to mind is shock. Also, we were worried about the men that were overseas and their safety. I regret that we were involved in the war and so many lives were lost."

What did you do for the war effort?

"When I was twenty-four years old, I started to work at Eli Lilly and Company in Indianapolis, Indiana. My job was record keeping for the raw materials that were used in the company. I worked there from 1942 to 1949." Eli Lilly and Company was a supplier of medicine for the troops that were fighting the war. Lilly produced the new penicillin drug that helped save many lives in WWII.

"Also, I helped to knit some diaper coverings to be sent overseas. They would have been used like rubber pants over the baby diaper which people during that time used."

Do you remember V-J Day?

"Yes, I heard on the radio that the war was over. I went down to Monument Circle in downtown Indianapolis. There were so many people that you couldn't move around.   Everyone was very happy that the war finally ended." V-J Day, or Victory over Japan, was on August 15, 1945. Japan formally surrendered and signed surrender papers aboard the USS *Missouri* at Pearl Harbor on September 2, 1945.

What do you want America to know about your experiences?

"It was a time of sacrifice, and it made everyone patriotic. There was a very patriotic feeling in the country."

What was your greatest achievement in your life?

"It would be having my husband, Richard, and my children, grandchildren and great-grandchildren in my life."

Lillian Beavers

Eli Lilly and Company, began by Colonel Eli Lilly in 1876, is a large pharmaceutical drug company headquartered in downtown Indianapolis, Indiana. A large supply of medicine was needed for sick and wounded soldiers as WWII continued. Penicillin, an important new antibiotic drug used to treat infections, was critically needed by the military.

What did you do for the war effort in WWII?

"I worked at Eli Lilly and Company filling capsules with penicillin. At this time there were no latex gloves, so vials had to be filled by hand. Women had always had this job. Since their hands were smaller than men's hands, they could do a better job at this task." They had so many capsules or vials to fill in an hour.

Top row – Betty, Lillian (mom), Dorothy, Gene (dad)
Bottom row – Lillian and Millie (sister)

What other things did you do for the military?

Many of the soldiers from Camp Atterbury and Fort Harrison were in the Indianapolis area since Indianapolis was a centrally located site for many of the men taking basic training or having been assigned to other military installations. Soldiers looked forward to having some social time at the various USO's around the United States. (Currently, the USO is still in service and provides breakfast for veterans taking Honor Flights to Washington D.C.) They have been a valuable service to the military for many years. "We went to dances at the USO and danced with the soldiers."

What did you do after you were married?

"After the war ended, I got married and had children."

Mildred "Smokey" Cummings

On December 7, 1941, Mildred was fifteen years old. "On Pearl Harbor day, I was in a car with three or four teenagers, and we went down to Crane Naval Base. We went down to see the lake; I imagine that we were the last ones to go through without a pass. I didn't find out about the Pearl Harbor attack until that evening. When I got home from the lake, my mother said, 'change your shoes, we are going to church.' I went to church, and they kept talking about something that I didn't understand. I finally got it; the war had started. After church was over, we went downtown (Bedford) to Hoovers, the high school hangout, where all the teenagers went to eat. We wondered about the war that was declared."

"In 1944, my high school boyfriend, Roy Cummings, was drafted while he was still in high school. He turned eighteen in January. They gave him a deferment until June, so he could graduate from high school. He then went to Louisville, Kentucky, to get his physical. As soon as he got that, he took a train to Chicago, Illinois Naval Station. The train came through Bedford, Indiana, around two or three o'clock in the morning. There were three cars loaded with guys going to Great Lakes Naval Training Station to enter the Navy. The guys were all shouting and yelling out the windows. I couldn't find my boyfriend, as I was walking up and down the platform. Finally, I found him hanging out the train window. Later in the war, Roy was in the landing on Omaha Beach in France." Mildred and Roy were married when he received a weekend pass in 1943, before he went overseas. They were married for thirty years.

What was your job during WWII?

"In 1943, after high school, I did some work at Reliance Manufacturing Company in Bedford, Indiana." It was a shirt factory that was located on 12th and K Street. "I sewed the white uniforms and the pants for the Navy. The company's main product was to make shirts, but during the war they made uniforms too. I worked there about three months. I didn't like the sewing but couldn't get another job in Bedford without a release. The company wouldn't give me a release because they needed me there."

"I really got myself in trouble because I couldn't get another job in Bedford, Indiana. The only thing I could do was to leave town. In late 1944, I moved in with my parents who were living in Knoxville, Tennessee. During this time, I would go with other women in the office shopping, bowling or to the movies. We would walk a lot as well. I lived with my parents for the rest of the time in Knoxville during 1944 and 1945."

"I found a job at a transportation company in Knoxville, Tennessee, Associated Transportation, that was transporting materials from various companies to Oak Ridge, Tennessee. The semis contained parts for the atomic bomb that were hauled to Oak Ridge." According to the Atomic Heritage Foundation website, "In 1942, General Leslie Groves approved Oak Ridge, Tennessee, as the site for the pilot plutonium plant and the uranium enrichment plant."

"On the waybill was a code. My job was to process the waybills. On the waybill it said Oak Ridge. At the time we didn't know what the code stood for. I stayed there for about a year and a half. It had Manhattan Project on the waybill; I thought we were doing something for New York City. I didn't know what this was all about. I was only eighteen and didn't know very much. When Roy came home from the military, I resigned from my job."

What happened when the war was over?

"A friend was visiting from Bedford, Indiana, and we went downtown Knoxville, Tennessee. People were celebrating the end of the war. There was a lot of noise and hullabaloo. They were beating on drums, and some people were singing. I mean there was just a mob, and they were doing everything. We liked it because we were excited too."

How did WWII affect you?

"I think about it a lot. I had two brothers, James and Edgar, in the Army. One was in Europe and the other was in North Africa, Italy, and Germany." Both of her brothers died at a very young age – forty-five and forty-eight, and Mildred blamed the war on their early deaths. "There was a lot to worry about in the war, but you couldn't dwell on it much. There were things in the newspaper about who was lost or killed. It was scary, but I was young. I think you take things better when you are young."

Did you see any famous people during this time?

"Yes, I did. My friend's father had a drugstore, and somehow, he got some tickets to this show. I did have a program, but I don't have it anymore. It was being performed at the University of Tennessee in the auditorium. The money went towards the war. I don't remember who was there. It was an hour and half program of singers and dancers."

What do you want America to know about your WWII experiences?

"As long as they know that we all pulled together during this time. This town (Bedford, Indiana) was empty of men. They took everybody, and there were very few that didn't pass the physical. That's one reason I liked going to Knoxville; at least there was some life down there. I don't know that I am anything special because I lived through it, but I tried to do my part. Another thing I did was sell war stamps on Saturdays. I wore my very best dress and sold stamps in front of the Woolworths store. These were the kind of stamps where you would buy war stamps for a dime and fill up a book. Then you turned the book in for a war bond. A couple other girls and I stood on the sidewalk and would try to sell them to people as they walked by to shop."

What was your greatest achievement in your life?

"I worked for the Department of the Navy, Crane Ammunition Depot, for a total of twenty years. Also, during that time I worked for the Navy base in the Philippines. I went over there for a two-year tour. When the two years were up, I felt like I was just getting started and knowing what I was doing; so, I signed up for two more years. I was over there for a total of four years."

What was your job in the Philippines?

"It was the same one that I had done at Crane hiring people for jobs on the base. For the first two years, I hired Americans to work in the Philippines and the second two-years, I hired Filipinos for jobs on the base. When I worked in the United States department, we hired people from the United States.

In the Philippines department, I hired Filipinos instead of Americans. That was a little more complicated. During this time, I was told it was the largest base in the Navy." The U.S. Navy base in Subic Bay closed in 1992.

"While in the Philippines, I lived on the base, and they had a lot going on all the time. There was entertainment and all. They wouldn't allow Americans to stay there longer than seven years. Some of the teachers taught at the American school and wanted to stay longer, but management wouldn't let them. I think management thought Americans would lose their Americanism. It was very interesting. I had a nice house with a maid. The maid even bathed the dog and took it for walks. I also had a seamstress. I got spoiled; life was easy. The Filipino people loved the Americans. The Filipinos were nice and would do anything they could to help you."

After Mildred's four years at Subic Bay Philippines Naval Base, she returned to Bedford, Indiana. "I came back to Crane to work. From there I went to Florida and worked at the submarine base in Georgia where I continued the same work

as I did at the other bases. Later, I retired from there." The Kings Bays Naval Submarine Base is located in southeast Georgia. The World Press website, states that "Kings Bay Naval Submarine Base represents the legacy of U.S. naval power during World War II."

Angie Timan and Smokey Cummings

Ruth Davis

How did WWII affect your life?

"It was a different life then: no television to tell us about the war, only radio. In 1941, I had just graduated from Warren Central High School. My husband, Maurice, graduated from Manual High School in Indianapolis, Indiana. We knew that he would be of the age for the military."

Do you remember the beginning of the war?

"Yes, we heard about it on the radio. We thought it was the end of the world in those days. We were married in December 1942, and in March 1943, Maurice was drafted into the 303rd Engineers Division of the Army. His job was to go before the infantry, and he was involved in the fighting in Germany. I didn't know anything about how much danger he was in until he came home. Right away, he went to Camp Butner, North Carolina, and had six weeks of training. I went down to be with him for a short time. Next, he went to New York for a short time and then overseas."

"I left our apartment and moved in with my parents. My dad had been in WWI, and my mother said, 'I can't believe we are going through this again. I know what you are going through.' Life was eight to five working and hoping when I got home there would be a letter from Maurice."

"The battles were going on and the engineers had some scary times. He didn't talk about the fighting very much. Of course, his letters were censored, so we didn't have much information about what was happening. My life was strictly my friends and planning what we would do when he got out of the Army. We didn't have a home at this point, since I was living with my parents."

"We were active in the church and many of my friends had husbands in the war. Our small group, Christian Endeavor, helped to support each other. It was a place where we could be with others who were going through the same thing that I was. I had one goal -- save my money. The church was very important to us. Since I lived at home and did not have to pay rent, we could have our own place when he got home. My dad said, 'I want you to take advantage of everything the government offers.' So, Maurice attended Butler University and graduated with a degree in Business, while I continued to work and support us. Later, Maurice went into the ministry."

What did you do for the war effort?

"I worked in the defense factory, Allison, in Indianapolis for about two years. I was one of the first ladies who went into the factory when the war started. My hours were from three to eleven, and I worked on a crankcase for the airplanes. It was a big piece of equipment that I pulled down the line. We put it on a table and made little holes in the sides. There were four holes in each end, and I fine-tapped it to fit just right on the airplane. I had to blow out the holes with an air gun. The crankcase was a large piece that fit into the airplane. I wore coveralls and a rubber apron for protection."

"These fine particles that were tapped off the crankcase were flying through the air. I became sick from the particles in the air. It was very heavy work. I developed a bad case of strep throat and could not recover from it. The only way I could get out of the job was to have a doctor's order. At that time, you could not quit a defense job. Then, I went to work at L.S. Ayres, a well-known department store in downtown Indianapolis, until Maurice came home."

What is an unexpected event that you recall?

"In 1942, while I was working at Allison, somebody was put on a machine who shouldn't have been placed there. The Union went on strike. I was working my job and didn't know what was going on. The Army came in, and we had to get out of the building. I rode the defense bus, and I couldn't get home. They let me stand way out of the way. This was during the war, and you didn't strike during the war. It only lasted that day, and everybody was back at work the next day. I was so young and didn't understand all that was going on. I thought, 'I didn't do anything.' They had placed a non-union person on a union job. Life was different then."

Do you remember the end of the war?

"That was all you talked about. When Maurice came home, we went to Camp Atterbury to get him. It was almost like I was frightened because I was going to face the actual person; he was almost like a stranger. I hadn't seen him in almost three years. It didn't take long for us to get acquainted again."

Group letter to Bob Poole from the Endeavor Group
which includes Ruth writing about husband, Maurice.

C. E. Hour
Southeastern Union
Church
August 22, 1943

Dear Bob,

Here we are again, spending the Christian Endeavor hour writing to boys in service. There are several yet to add a line to this note, so I'll send it on. Esther

Hello Bob,

Guess what? Maurice is on his way home. I am thrilled beyond words, so I will just say hello, and best of luck

Ruth Allen Lewis

Bob, dear,

There isn't much left for me to write now, since I wrote you a nice long letter this afternoon. I'm almost excited as Ruth about Maurice's coming home. Can't imagine how I will live through it when word comes that you are on the way.

Love,
Betty

"All we knew was what he could write in a letter and the news on the radio. His division was trying to find the enemy, and he was shot at by the Germans several times. At that time, the only news you found out about the war was from him or the newspapers. Life was at a standstill. You got the newspaper, but you didn't get the face-to-face news like we do today."

What do you want America to know about your experiences?

"I can't imagine that this would ever happen again. I want America to know that we have to stand firm. Of course, my religion says, 'It's God's plan.' For me, sometimes it's better not knowing too much. We, who were active in a church, put our arms around each other with a strong hold. We were all going through the same thing together."

What was your greatest achievement in your life?

"I was never able to have children. We were just about ready to start the adoption process when Paul and Roger, Maurice's nephews, came to live with us. The boys' mother had been a widow for several years before she died. At the time, both the boys were in grade school, so Maurice and I took them to raise."

Rosalind "Linda" Faraday

"Before WWII, I had just graduated from college, and in that summer, the Civil Aeronautics Authority offered women the opportunity to learn to fly. I think they wanted to know if women could learn to fly. I went to Babylon, Long Island which was a seaport. I lived on Long Island, New York. I was one of fifteen women who all got our licenses flying Piper Cub seaplanes. I made a solo cross-country flight over water. I did three different landings, and there was someone at each landing to validate it. It was really an experience. When you are that young, nothing is daring."

What did you do for the war effort?

"In December 1941, the war started, and I went to work at Grumman Aircraft. I installed aileron gear boxes in cockpits of Grumman F4F airplanes. I didn't rivet them, but screwed them in. I worked in the aircraft factory several months before I met my husband, James, who was in the military." According to History Net website, "the Grumman F4F Wildcat was a U.S. Navy fighter in World War II." The article describes the F4F airplane as "a heroic airplane."

A similar aircraft was the Grumman Bearcat.

Photo courtesy of Tom Wood Aviation

How did you meet your husband?

"What is interesting about this is that I had a subscription to Carnegie Hall. My school friend and I had gone every Sunday afternoon to the concerts and sat in the balcony. My future husband, Jim, and I met on a blind date at Carnegie Hall. When I met him, we were seated in a box. We took it from there. We were married right away in September 1943. He served in India and flew over the hump into China. As a result of that trip, he lost the hearing in one ear, and the military sent him home."

How did WWII affect your life?

"It affected my life in every way. One way was having my husband overseas. One of the places he had been stationed was in Manhattan, but he came back to the west coast. I thought I wanted to try California, and so he was ultimately stationed in San Francisco. He later retired as a full colonel. Once you are in California, you don't go back to New York."

What is your greatest regret about you time during WWII?

"I have no regrets."

What do you want America to know about your experiences?

"I am glad that I had the experience because that is part of my life, so I know what went on during the war. I was in my early twenties during that time. Our whole focus was on saving the United States."

Susanna Smith Lautzenheiser

Susanna, nicknamed Su, wanted to stress the importance of what the environment was during this time in the 1940's. "It was war time when I graduated from high school in 1944. America had been in the war since the end of 1941. At home it was peaceful, compared to today's environment; it was almost idyllic. I lived in Wichita, Kansas, the second largest city in the state. Kansas City was the largest. There were three major aircraft factories in Wichita - Boeing, Beechcraft, and Cessna. Another thing, there was no unemployment because there was such a drive to support the war effort. You heard a lot about supporting the war effort, such as doing your job, make the best product you can produce, and good morale. Also, there was the phrase, 'a slip of the lips sinks ships.' This was around everywhere – in the grocery store, ice cream store, or drugstore."

"My father, Bill Smith, also worked at Boeing until the war was over. My mother, Fern Smith, worked at Cessna. Her job at the Cessna plant was as a seamstress. The wings of the planes were covered in a canvas fabric. My mother didn't work there very long because the men were not very nice. The country was so mobilized producing instruments of war, i.e. the Crayola factory started making bullets – both about the same size and shape."

What was your position or job?

"The people from the factories came to the high schools and solicited employees. I don't know if there were other employers, but I signed up with Boeing. During this time, they were making B-29 airplanes. The B-29 was huge, but not luxurious. The soldier had to crawl through a narrow space. There was a belly turret on it. The finished planes were parked out on the parking lot, and it was a big thrill to me to see them. I crawled through the planes, but I never flew in one. That was before graduation, and when you graduated, the company had some type of agreement for you to go to work."

"After graduation, we were sent to Lawrence, Kansas, which is where Kansas University is located. We found our own housing which was approved by the university. I rented a room with a girlfriend; we went to classes, did several things in a trade school part of the university and operated some machines. We were taught about materials and design of aircraft, about structure, stress of materials, and related subjects."

"Then after six or eight weeks, we went back to Wichita to the factory. I think my job had a title, but I don't recall what it was. I worked out of an office. Every part that was manufactured had a number and a file card. As it was being assembled, that tub and its card would follow those parts to the final assembly. I followed around those parts that were frequently lost. My job was to track down the missing parts. The parts almost always were found. Often they had been mislabeled or sent to the wrong location."

"The factory ran two shifts, ten hours a day. The day shift and the night shift were set for five days a week. I guess the factory rested the other four hours a day. Before I quit, my salary increased to fifty cents an hour. I thought I was really rich. I had to work the day shift because I was only seventeen years old. I rode to work in a car pool. The driver got an extra ration for gas and tires. A lot of people who worked there knew that it was a temporary job. I don't think it was a career. I worked there approximately one year. This was about the end of June 1944 to June 6, 1945."

How did you meet your husband?

"In July of 1945, my friend and I went to Pasadena, California on the train to enroll at Pasadena Junior College. Incidentally, the queen of the Rose Bowl Parade was always selected from that college then. I worked full time and went to school part time." Su started working at the telephone company. "During the train trip, we met a soldier named Earl at breakfast in the dining car. All military personnel were in uniform because it was a court-martial offense to be out of uniform in public. Therefore, soldiers and sailors were easy to recognize. After breakfast, my friend and I weren't in a hurry, so we sat down to talk to him. He told me how to pronounce his name, as his ancestors were from Germany. Earl was on his way to Santa Ana Air base where he was stationed. He gave me his address, and I wrote a post card to him after we had secured housing. Kate Smith and many of the entertainers said, 'If you don't write, you are wrong.' You should write to the servicemen. It was very common for people to do this. In a week or so, he called and we had a date."

"After three or four times, he came to see me; my friend Dean told Earl that he didn't need to come back unless he had a friend for her. Earl was discharged in October. He hadn't been home for Christmas since 1941 because he was in the Army. Earl's mother wanted him to come home for Christmas, December 1945." On December 3rd, Earl and Su were married. "I had written my mother that I was going to get a ride to Wichita; that I had a friend who was coming. I hadn't told her that I was married. I just knocked on the door and said, 'This is my husband.' I think it was terrible; however, my mother was cool with it. Earl's brother offered him a job, and we moved to Indiana."

What was your greatest achievement in your life?

"My greatest achievement was my six children, also, going to college after my children were almost grown." She graduated from Ball State University in 1974 with an education degree.

How did WWII affect your life?

"Number one, that's how I met Earl. This was a period of time when people traveled more. Before this time, you married the people that were around you, especially the people who lived in the rural areas. During WWII, that custom changed with train travel." During the war, "coffee, sugar, meat, butter, and shoes were rationed; other things were not rationed, but just scarce to get. It didn't seem like a hardship in this country. Housing was scarce, so people who had never rented a room, or part of their house, did so to make space for people during the war years."

What do you want America to know about your experiences and life during WWII?

"I just want to convey that it was a calm time at home. Of course, families had been separated. Some had lost loved ones. The whole country listened to the war news and prayed for the men overseas. Everybody who wanted to work was working. Crime and violence were way down. Most people didn't lock their car doors or houses. They say that if there was four percent unemployment, then there is full employment."

Do you remember when the war was over?

"In August 1945, I decided to take the trolley to Los Angeles, California, to shop. I was in the store when I heard, 'The war is over. The war is over.' News spread like wildfire through the store. Everybody ran out into the street. They closed the store, and I was all by myself. I decided to go back to Pasadena; it was standing room only on the trolley. The next day I went back to work."

"When the war ended, many ex-military people came home and established new families. Jobs were plentiful because manufacturing was raging. So many things were needed because their production had been delayed due to the war. The housing shortage was even more acute during this time. There was so much unity during this time. It was hard to be a civilian single man because the girls flocked to a uniform. Manufacturing had been delayed, and it was very difficult to buy a new refrigerator and many other appliances. Cars were very scarce. When they did make new cars, it wasn't a new model year. For example, in 1943 and 1944, it was the same model car as 1942. Gasoline and tires were rationed, so there wasn't a lot of driving for pleasure."

Helen Dougherty Anderson McClellan

How did WWII affect your life?

At age nineteen, Helen Dougherty married Earl Anderson September 5, 1942. "We knew at the time we were married he would probably be drafted into the service. We were a little nervous about it because of what was going on in Germany. When Pearl Harbor happened, we knew the United States was going to get into the war. Earl was called up January 1, 1943 and was classified as "Four F" because of how bad his kidneys had become." Earl experienced many illnesses during their marriage, but the most damaging one to his body was the continuing kidney disease. He was treated many times at the Mayo Clinic; however, he continued to be ill due to his failing kidneys. "During World War II, Earl worked with an electrician for about four months."

"My husband's grandparents came from Germany. They stowed away on a ship and eventually located to North Dakota. Earl's mother lived in North Dakota and cooked for the chuckwagons. My father was working at New York Central Railroad because there was a shortage of men due to the war. My dad knew the general foreman in the storeroom at the Beech Grove Shops, Indianapolis, Indiana, and put in a word for me. I went for an interview and was hired as an "Office Boy". I carried mail to all the shops around the railroad shops, such as the forge shop, mill room, freight ship and back to the store room. I thought I would never find my way around."

"About eleven days after I got the job as mail boy, there was a job opening in the office as a clerk: posting invoices, filing all the papers from invoices, and anything that had to be filed. We ordered materials for the roundhouses. The roundhouses are where the workers repair the trains. I worked in the purchasing department."

The railroad was an important means of transportation during WWII. Some of the freight bills that Helen filed were for the war department and meant that war supplies would be transported to where they were needed. "There were a lot of troop trains. We could get passes to ride the train, since we worked on the railroad. One time we couldn't get a seat because there were so many military personnel on the train. The soldiers mixed with the passengers too."

"There was rationing, especially gasoline. You had a hard time getting very much of it. My husband lived close to Bedford, Indiana, when we were dating, and he came to Indianapolis to stay with his brother Ralph. He had to hitchhike to get here."

What do want America to know about your experiences during WWII?

"It was a tough time because of rationing, and there were not many enjoyable things to do. We did go to the movies. There would be newsreels about the war and to buy war bonds. We were afraid that maybe the fighting might come over here. We were sorry for the fellas in the service. We had a friend, Clifton Short, who was a prisoner of war who was very skinny when he returned. Also, a cousin Howard Grindstaff was a prisoner of war and lost a lot of weight. Another friend Jack McClellan was in the Navy and worked on an aircraft carrier repairing planes." Many years later after Earl died, Helen married Jack McClellan.

What did your family do to help the war effort?

"Sugar was hard to get, and my mother canned food. I canned food and had a victory garden."

What is your greatest achievement in your life?

"My greatest achievement was my children." Helen's daughter Donna died from cancer in 2008. Helen said it was, "the saddest day of my life."

What is a regret from this time?

"I had to go to work and had to leave my children many times. I felt like I could have contributed more to the war effort. The church, Acton Baptist Church, made bandages for the war effort."

Clara Elizabeth "Betty" Short

Clara, nicknamed Betty by her family, does not go by Clara. In 1944, she began working at Allison Plant 3 in Speedway, Indiana. According to the Allison War Album, "Allison was the principal powerplant for fighter planes of the U.S. Army Air Forces and was widely used by other United Nations. Allison produced engines for these planes: the P-38 Lightnings, the P-39 Airacobra, the P-51a Mustang, and in the P-40 Tomahawks, Kittyhawks, and Warhawks. War-wise fliers praised them." Allison is still doing business today in Indiana.

What was your job at Allison?

"I ran lathes and drills just as the men did before the men left for the war. Allison was making airplane motors during this time. I did more burr work than anything else. I would use a burr gun to sand down the rough spots using sandpaper. You had to take a hand machine to smooth it out. I was there for a year and a half before the war ended. When the war ended, so did my job. They needed the jobs for the men returning from the war. During the war, I made forty-four cents an hour. We worked long hours and seven days a week. We worked from 6:30 a.m. to 3 p.m. and worked a lot of overtime too. We did whatever needed to be done. I could not quit my war defense job and get another job for six months. The government wanted people to work, and I was glad to help the war effort."

"During the time that I worked at the plant, the company sold war bonds. They had celebrities and bands that came into the plant to sell war bonds. The company helped the war efforts by sponsoring blood drives. I had several war bonds that I purchased from Allison. We were able to see the completed engines run. We went to a special room where they tested them."

"Before the war, when I was sixteen years old, I worked for the Real Silk Hosiery Mills on Noble Street. I worked piece work there; I was paid by the piece for seventeen cents an hour. After the war started, the company converted to making parachutes for the military. Many years later, the company moved to Mexico."

After the war~

"When the soldiers came home from the war, they couldn't find a place to live. I lived in an apartment on New Jersey Street. When some soldiers came to the door, I told them that if they would buy my furniture, they could have the apartment. I had been dating Merrill for four or five years. In 1943, he came home on a furlough from the National Guard – 39th Field Artillery, and we were married. Many years later, my son said, 'Why did you get married on a furlough?' I said, 'He might have been killed if we waited.' When the war ended in 1945, my husband returned from the war. We moved in with my husband's parents. I became pregnant and quit my job. I had a few bonds which I sold, and my husband, Merrill, bought a car with the money. In 1946, my daughter Linda was born."

How did WWII affect your life?

"They rationed everything. You got tickets, and if you had lots of tickets on hosiery, we would trade to get something else we needed. People didn't mind doing that."

"I don't think I ran out of anything; we just learned to live without things. For example, you couldn't get refrigerators, but I got one somehow. I guess I got a 'black market' one. We were always worried about our men and hoped they would get back safely."

What do you want America to know about your experiences?

"Get out there and honor the flag, and don't be afraid to say the Pledge of Allegiance like they are now...some of them. It doesn't seem right to me because people should appreciate America and having freedom. I don't understand that because I have always appreciated America."

What was your greatest achievement in your life?

"I had four children, and they are my greatest achievement."

Carla Sorrelle

Do you remember the bombing of Pearl Harbor?

"Oh, yes. It was about two o'clock in the afternoon in Cincinnati, Ohio. We were just cleaning up from Sunday dinner and had the radio on. Dad called us into the living room and said, 'Listen to this.' It was the bombing of Pearl Harbor. He happened to know where Pearl Harbor was because my uncle was in the Navy at that time. He had been stationed at Pearl and dad knew immediately. It was a shock. The next day at school, classes were suspended when President Roosevelt gave his famous speech."

"Yesterday, December 7, 1941 – a date which will live in infamy – the United States of America was suddenly and deliberately attacked by naval and air forces of the empire of Japan." www.usatoday.com

"When I met Jack, I was a freshman in high school, and he was a junior. We both loved to dance, and our friendship blossomed into romance. He was nineteen, and I was eighteen when we eloped in August 1944."

What was your job or position?

"In the summer of 1945, the war in Europe was over, but we were still fighting in the Pacific. When I was nineteen, I went to work for the Lodge & Shipley Machine Tool Company in Cincinnati, Ohio. They made pumps for the Navy."

"I worked in the drafting room; I was a tracer. In those days, the engineers made the plans, and we tracers would trace them off, so they could be duplicated and passed out. The plans were linen dipped in a blue solution of some kind. We traced from that, and I think, it was a mimeograph that was used to copy these."

"I did this from eight to four for five days a week for the summer months during college. I rode the streetcar to downtown Cincinnati. I worked in the drafting room which was over the factory; it was hotter than Hades since there was no air conditioning. I worked there about three and a half months. The university that I attended had a co-op system, and the drafting room was one of their co-ops. So, the university let me have the job for the summer. Normally, students would go to school for six weeks and then work for six weeks to pay for their tuition. This was how the co-op worked."

"The engineers would give me three or four blueprints at a time. They would never give you a whole plan at once. It looked like gears and things that went into pumps. I had a set of special pens that I used to trace on this vellum. When I finished it, I would turn it in and start the next one. When I ran out of blueprints, the engineers would give me four more. We had a thirty-minute break for lunch at eleven-thirty, and then we would work until four. I had architectural drawing my first year in college, so that gave me the opportunity to do this. I remember the pay being very good. It was rewarding to be able to do what I could for the war effort. Later, I attended the University of Kentucky and earned a degree in Psychology."

How did WWII affect your life?

"It really affected it greatly because my husband, John (Jack), was overseas in Europe and flew B-26s. He flew thirty-five missions and had two crash landings. Thankfully, he came home in one piece. When he came home, he had three years of college left. He got out of the military and went to school on the GI Bill. I transferred to where he was going to college, and I always said, 'We were roommates,' even though we were married at the time."

"Everyone was affected by the rationing during the war, especially of sugar. Before Jack went overseas, he came home on leave. The woman who worked for his mother gave her a bag of sugar so that his mother could make a birthday cake for Jack. Sugar was very tight. Soap, meat, butter and gasoline were rationed, and we had ration cards. This is when oleo came in. Ugh! It was terrible stuff that you had to add color to the mixture. It was really a big deal."

What do you remember about when the war ended?

"When my husband Jack came home on the Queen Mary, they arrived in New York harbor at the conclusion of the war. They were well greeted with all kinds of music and streamers. He said there was a brassiere factory near where the ship came into the harbor. All the girls were leaning out the factory windows waving brassieres at them when they arrived."

"My friends were overseas or coming home at this time. I was very much into the news and what was going on with the war. My husband was recalled in 1951 for the Korean War. His training in WWII and his recall in Korean War affected my life."

What was your greatest achievement in your life?

"My greatest achievement was being an Air Force wife and raising two great kids. Our son went into the military and spent six years flying F-4s."

What do you think about women in the military and their achievements?

"I have known several WASPs, Women Air Service Pilot, and it really influenced their lives. I would have loved to have been one, but I was not qualified at the time. I thought they were super. My husband and I met a WASP in Japan, and he was shocked to hear that she had more B-26 time than he did. She had ferried airplanes, and she had a lot of time in the air. The WASPs were a leading group of women for their time. Women in the military were a very new thing in WWII. Of course, you had a group of young girls around a lot of men, so families worried about them. I never heard of any problems; I think it worked out well."

What do you want America to know about your experiences?

"We live in the greatest country in the world. Without a doubt, our system is the best, and I have lived around the world. I kiss the ground I walk on when I get home. During WWII, it was rewarding to know that you could do something to help the war effort. We bought war bonds that eventually matured. In high school, every Monday morning they sold stamps which were put into a small book. The stamps were about ten or fifteen cents each. My dad was a block warden. Even in Cincinnati they would practice black outs. He would walk around and make sure that everybody had their lights out, and it was dark."

"I can remember toward the end of the war, the first jets flying overhead. What a surprise that was. When you heard the noise, it was different. You would look in the wrong place. By this time the jets were way ahead of the where you were looking. Dayton, Ohio, was our closest military base. Jack talked about the first German jets, how scary they were, and the different missions he went on."

"Jack met the German pilot that shot down his plane. We went to a reunion in Arlington, Texas, and there was a reproduction of a painting. This German pilot was there, and the picture just happened to be of Jack's last mission. The German pilot claimed Jack as a kill. In the picture, there is a B-26 going down, but Jack hit the treetops and was able to stabilize the plane and land it. The pilot happened to be in the picture. He was the one flying the German 109 plane. The German pilot and my husband, Jack, realized they had a connection. Somewhere in the conversation, Jack said, 'I lost my best friend on this mission.' The German pilot said, 'I lost one too, and he was my brother.' They both hugged each other and had tears in their eyes. That was Jack's last mission; Jack and the crew survived, but the plane didn't. He never lost a crew member in his flights. Both times he crash-landed, he was able to get across enemy lines to an American field. I just knew he would be okay and come home from the war."

What was a funny or unexpected event that happened when Japanese surrendered at end of the war?

"I happened to be visiting relatives on August 14, 1945, in Fairfax, Missouri. My grandmother and some aunts and uncles lived there. My mother had gone out earlier, and I stayed home because I was working until I had a two-week break; then I went out too. My two little brothers and I went to the village and the sirens went off. My uncle happened to be the volunteer fireman of the village. So, he immediately went to the firehouses to get the wagons out. I happened to be across the street with these two little boys, and my uncle said, 'Help me, somebody help me.' Everybody was laughing so hard they couldn't take time to explain. Finally, someone told him that the war was over and that was why the sirens were going off. It was a good laugh, and one the family remembers today."

Another humorous time at the end of the war involved her parents. "My mother's name was Mary Martin. Since my dad didn't take any vacations, he stayed in Cincinnati. The victory party was at mother and dad's house. He went ahead and opened the house and prepared for the party. One of the guests worked for the telephone company. The guest decided to call mother, but the lines were tied up. He got on the phone with a special operator, and said he was calling Mary Martin. The operator asked, 'Does she sing?' and he said, 'Of course, she sings.' Then the call went though. There were many family and friends who came to the party."

Carla recalled some not funny events. "I lost an uncle who was in the Navy and was killed in the Pacific in a submarine. I lost a great friend who was on a LST during the D-Day invasion on Day Three. Another friend was the president of our senior high school class. He was eighteen, an only child, and was going to be drafted. His dad wanted him to wait and join the Air Force. He waited and was drafted into the Army; six weeks later he was killed. That death was very sad. Those were tough times that you remember until today."

Ruby Hasselburg Warmouth

Ruby Hasselburg married Jim Warmouth on November 20, 1941. Life changed for everyone on December 7th when the Japanese bombed Pearl Harbor. Jim enlisted in the U.S. Army Infantry. He fought in Germany, Switzerland, and England during the war. Jim returned home in January 1946.

What was your job at Eli Lilly and Company during the war?

"I worked in the plasma or blood bank at Eli Lilly and Company in Indianapolis, Indiana, and we sent plasma to the boys overseas. I had several different jobs. I would label the plasma and get it ready to send to the various hospitals to save our boys' lives. Also, we used to send cookies and fudge to the servicemen overseas in the plasma containers. We sealed them up in the plasma can. It was my boss' idea."

"The blood would come in, and we had to get it ready to send overseas. It would be put in centrifuges and processed. My job was usually in the finishing of the process. After the war ended, the blood bank at Lilly didn't last much longer. I was sent to other areas of the company to work. I worked for Eli Lilly and Company for twenty-two years."

How did WWII affect your life?

"Jim and I were separated for probably four years because of the war. We had a son, and it was very rough. You had to be careful with the letters you wrote, and the soldiers had to be careful with the letters they sent to us. We had ration books that we had to use."

After the war...

After WWII, Ruby's husband, Jim, was the secretary of the 75th division for thirty-five years. "Jim's division, called the Diaper Division, was one of the youngest groups that went over. The men were recruited right out of college, and some didn't have any training. After the war, some of these men were seeing each other for the first time since the war ended. They would actually cry; we became a large family."

Rolling bandages after the war~

"In 1946, our neighborhood got together and rolled bandages. We had a nurse that lived behind us who headed up the group. We send bandages to different places overseas. We got together once a week at different houses. Everybody would donate materials because we didn't have any money then. People didn't have anything in Europe after the war, and they needed medical supplies."

"The 75th helped the town of Colmar, Germany, which was heavily bombed and needed supplies. Jim made friends with different people in Europe and knew they needed help. After the war, the 75th helped people in the war zone. In 1970, I started going to Europe, and it was something to see. The 75th donated an ambulance to this area. I made seven trips to Europe after the war with my husband and other veterans."

What do you want America to know about your experience?

"I think it makes you closer to your husband. We made a lot of very good friends who were war veterans." In 2011, Jim died, and Ruby received letters from his buddies after Jim's death. All the war materials were sent to a Texas museum which houses all the items bought home from the war. There are several widows still living from that group.

What was your greatest achievement in your life?

"My achievement in my life was helping children. I was very active in the Ladies Shrine, and we did a lot for the children in the hospital. We raised money for them and did sewing. The money we raised went to the Shrine Hospitals to help the children. I have taught over a hundred kids to swim, and my house was an open house for kids. I helped a young man Jimmy who was sleeping in my garage. I brought him into my home and kept him for several years. My life has been a wonderful life."

Author Note~

Sadly, after an admirable life helping others, Ruby passed away in March 2018.

Marion Wynn

"During the Depression, my dad was working for the WPA, Work Projects Administration, for sixty-nine dollars a month. There were eleven children in the family, and I was third from the oldest. In 1942, I was living in Minnesota. One day my dad saw an ad in the Minnesota paper stating that anyone who wanted to work in the shipyards in California, Kaiser would pay their way out on the train. He talked it over with my mother, and she agreed to stay at home and take care of the children if he wanted to work in California. They had just lost a baby. One of our babies had died and my brother had joined the service, but we still had nine children at home. My dad got two friends of the family to go to California with him."

"When my dad and his friends got to California, they couldn't find a place with three beds. So, they rented a place with one bed and each of them worked a different shift; they slept in the same bed at different times. When they each had saved enough money, they bought a trailer house and moved into the same trailer park."

"In 1943, Dad came home for a visit. My older sister had quit school, so he told her she could go back to California with him. I cried because I wanted to go, too. My dad told me if I didn't finish high school, I couldn't come at all. I had one year left to go, so I finished high school in 1944. I was seventeen, and my girlfriend and I took the Greyhound Bus to Mankato, Minnesota, to find a job."

"We found a job bagging granulated rock-wool insulation for fifty-three cents an hour. It took us two months to save enough money to go to California. I went home to celebrate my eighteenth birthday with my mother and my eight brothers and sisters. While I was there, the military came out and told us my brother Donald Parsons was killed at Normandy. I stayed a few more days with my mom, then left for California in a Greyhound Bus. The bus traveled at the posted speed limit of thirty-five miles per hour. I arrived in California the end of August 1944 and was going to stay with my dad."

What was your job or position?

"When I got to California, my dad took me to the hiring hall. They were hiring welders, and I got a job as a pipe fitter. I went to school for two weeks to learn how to weld. The first thing the instructor said was, 'There are three things you need to remember: the size of your pipe, the size of the rod needed to weld that pipe, and the amount of heat needed to weld the pipe.' If it was too hot, it would burn a hole in the pipe. If too cold, it would stick to the pipe. We worked in an area called West Storage on the outskirts of Yard Three."

"Eleven women did the welding there every day. We made one dollar an hour. We had men who set up the pipes for us and when the men took them away, they took them to the ship all assembled and ready to put in place on the ship. I worked weekends on the ship, tacking handrails in place. I wasn't qualified to weld the handrails, but I could tack them in place, so when the welders came in on Monday, they could weld them in place. I was paid one dollar and fifty cents an hour on Saturday and two dollars an hour on Sunday. I only worked on the ship on weekends. I worked every weekend I could to help my dad with the little ones at home."

"Kaiser had a small Field Hospital outside the shipyard on Cutting Blvd. Workers went there for more severe wounds than could be cared for at the first aid station inside the yard. For the more serious wounds or illnesses, workers went to the large hospital in Oakland. The field hospital was open twenty-four hours a day. One time I got slag in my eye and had to go to the field hospital on Cutting Blvd."

"I had to wear a leather jacket, leather overalls, gloves to my elbows, and men's lace up high-top shoes with steel toes. We had our hair tied up in a bandana with a welding hood over that. The war was winding down, and my dad had gone back home."

"We weren't making anymore new ships, so we had to help finish the ones already made. One day my girlfriend and I were welding a seam on one side of the hold of the ship. The workers were chipping out some bad welds on the other side of the hold. There was so much noise we couldn't stand it. My friend yelled at me that she was going home at noon. I yelled back that I was too. Our boss, standing in the door, came over and told us, 'You know what will happen if you go home.' We told him we didn't care because we couldn't stand that noise for another four hours, so we went home."

"I went back on Monday morning, and my boss said, 'What are you doing here'? I said, 'I came back to finish my job.' He said, 'You don't have a job; remember you went home Friday.' So, I had quit my job. I said, 'okay.'"

"I went to the cannery to put in an application, and they hired me. I had worked in a cannery in Minnesota when I was sixteen, so I had the experience. Three weeks later the war was over, and I still had a job. If I had stayed at the shipyard, I would not have had a job."

"When I first came to California, my dad didn't want me to go with any of the men in the shipyard. I met my future husband, Lloyd Wynn, who was in the Navy as soon as I got there. We got acquainted and went together for seven months before getting married in May 1945. My husband had just transferred from New York to Treasure Island. We were married for sixty years until he passed away in 2005."

How did WWII affect your life?

"Well, it helped us to have some money. We were so poor with eleven children in our family. My mom would buy two sacks of flour with the print of the same kind, and when the flour was gone, we would use the flour sacks to make a dress. The material from the two flour sacks would make a dress or whatever was needed. I was making my own dresses by age fourteen. The neighbors would all get together and have a sewing bee. They would buy a bolt of flannel and make pajamas or nightgowns for the children. Just as a note, we used the pieces of metal from the coffee cans that had key cans. My dad cut the pieces of metal the right length, and we rolled our hair on them to make it curly. We used the empty molasses container for our lunch boxes. We raised potatoes and rutabagas. My dad would take them to trade for something else we could use."

Where were you when the war ended?

"I was working at the cannery when suddenly all the whistles started blowing and all the machinery shut down. People were screaming and there was chaos. I couldn't wait to go home to tell my husband the war was over. I had to go to a pay phone and wait my turn. By the time I got to call him, and he answered the phone, I could tell by the background noise, he already knew. There was screaming, and I could hardly hear him. He was in the Naval Hospital in Oakland, California, following surgery on his hand. I was happy because I knew he would be coming home."

What was a funny or unusual event that happened during this time?

"This happened before I met my husband. We were rationed for everything, and I only had one stamp left for shoes. My dad dropped me off in town and went home to fix dinner. I told the salesman that I only had one more stamp left, so I wanted to get a good pair. He said, 'I will give you a stamp, if you will go out with me.' I said, 'no, thanks.' When I went home, I told my dad. My dad said, 'Are you going out with him'? I said, 'No, he's too old. I don't know; he must be thirty-four.' At that time, I thought thirty-four was ancient."

What do you want America to know about your experiences?

"I think everybody should try anything. If you want to get a job, try it. A lot of people say I could never have done that. Well, you didn't try it. You have to try it. I think a lot more people would be happier if they would try to do what they wanted to do. I have worked all my life."

Do you have any regrets about this time?

"No, I have more happy times than regrets. This was during the time I met my husband. I wish I would have gotten a job where I received a pension."

What was your greatest achievement in your life?

"I think finding a man that I could live with forever. Having a daughter, grandchildren, and great-grandchildren and a home that is paid for are great achievements. I don't have too much to worry about because I have had a happy life."

Rosie the Riveter~

"There are still several of the women who worked in the shipyards who are still working together at the Rosie the Riveter Visitors Center." Three of the Rosies, Kay Morrison, Marian Sousa, and Marian Wynn, travel together to talk about their time at Richmond Kaiser Shipyard Number Three. "The Rosies are working at the park where Yard Number Two used to be. The National Park Service in Richmond, California, has a Visitors Center and the Rosies volunteer there."

WOMEN ON THE HOME FRONT

Women have held an important place in American history since Betsy Ross. When WWII broke out in 1941, many American women proved they could help support the war effort on the home front. According to the Khan Academy, a non-profit educational organization, "approximately 350,000 American women joined the military during WWII. They worked in the medical field, drove trucks, repaired airplanes, and performed clerical work to free up men for combat." However, many women could not leave home to join the military and contributed by supporting the men overseas. The home front workers were vital to the success and comfort of our fighting men. Home front women wrote letters to servicemen, staffed the USO centers, and sent care packages to lonely soldiers.

The war required the production of war materials. Women proved they were physically able and intellectually equal to men; however, they still wanted to be feminine. The Khan Academy stated, "some factories gave female employees lessons in how to apply makeup and cosmetics were never rationed during the war. Keeping American women looking their best was believed to be important for morale."

Betty Burton

Do you remember the beginning of the war?

"I was on a date with a fellow, and when he came back to the car, he said, 'The Japanese have attacked Pearl Harbor.' War is terrible." The United States declared war on Japan on December 8, 1941.

How did WWII affect your life?

"There was rationing of gasoline, so many people were not able to travel long distances. I remember gasoline cost sixteen or seventeen cents a gallon. My family owned a grocery store in Morgan county, Indiana, and my dad would load the truck with some of the things in the store, such as bags of sugar, some chickens, eggs, or other supplies that families would need and deliver items to families. The truck was called a Huckster truck which had shelves along the side for the food supplies and general merchandise. Often, either my mom or I would go along with my dad. People would barter with each other. For example, if you needed eggs and someone else needed sugar, you would trade items. I wonder how many new recipes were created as we had to use the coupons for many items."

"My brother, Russell Sunderland, graduated from high school; then he was on a train for Great Lakes Naval Station. Nothing was as difficult as seeing loved ones go off to war, praying for their safe return." However, life continued for the people on the home front. "When I got out of school, I would walk to where my mother worked, and my mom and I would go to White Castle. You could get six hamburgers for twenty-five cents."

"My dad would drop me off at my piano lesson on the way  into town sometimes. We had to combine trips to save gasoline. The roads in the country were dirt roads which were a mess. The county workers would spray oil on the roads to keep the dust down. It was a time to make do with what you had. I remember my mom making a cake one time without sugar because we had used up our ration points."

"We didn't always have money to buy new shoes, so my dad would put cardboard in the soles of our shoes. It helped to extend the life of the shoes. When we bought new shoes, they were about three sizes too large, so they would last longer. Having a pair of nylons was a prize, so many evenings were spent in repairing and sewing up the runs."

"During my junior year in high school, I worked for a family as a nanny. I attended Howe High School that year. For my senior year in high school, I returned home and graduated from Monrovia High School."

"My dad was a cruel man but provided for the five children in the family. I wanted to attend college to become a teacher. He would not help me to become a teacher; instead he wanted me to go to work as a secretary. I tried to do as my father told me to do, so I didn't go to college then. Eventually, I went to college and became a third-grade teacher."

Do you remember the end of the war?

"There were a lot of celebrations. There was sadness because some of the families had lost sons in the war. We did a lot of praying and shed a lot of tears. My cousin Bill lost his life during the war. WWII changed our way of life in America. Even though the assembly line was already developed, it was improved with the constant need of war supplies to fight the war."

What did your family do for the war effort?

"Our family bought war bonds, and I bought war bonds even after the war was over. We tried to use what we had and were not wasteful with things."

What do you want America to know about your experiences during this time?

"I think there is a similarity between the Jewish immigrants of WWII and the way immigrants are being treated today. The United States would not allow the Jewish immigrants into our country when they were trying to escape persecution in Europe. It is happening today in the United States."

What was the greatest achievement in your life?

"I am thankful that I have a good relationship with all my family. We get together every Thanksgiving and spend time with each other. My husband, Jack, and I were married in 1949 and had two children. My husband's mother was an old-fashioned woman who thought that men should take care of women. So, we were married and didn't tell anyone for a while. The greatest achievement in my life would be my children and my marriage to Jack."

Imogene Wilcoxson Emmert

Do you remember the beginning of the war?

"Yes, I was in the eighth grade on December 7, 1941, and we lived in Indianapolis. We had a little table model Crosley radio, and we heard about the attack. We had the radio on almost all day. The radio gave this message – Important news: Pearl Harbor has been bombed by the Japanese. Then, the next day, I remember more vividly because we listened to President Roosevelt declare war on Japan; it was a sad time. You didn't think about what your plans were for next week, or tomorrow; you just thought about today."

"We were a family with six children, which I helped to care for being the oldest child. My mother, Helen, had severe asthma especially during the summer. To help out the family, I learned to cook and sew, and made most of my clothes for school. I used printed sacks to make dirndle skirts, which had two side seams. You gathered the skirt and put a band and button on it."

"My father, Oliver Wilcoxson, had not worked for quite a while during the Depression, and he was a union man. As factories were trying to keep the unions out, or under control, he lost a good job because of the union. So, we were all scared, but he was hired at Allison. When my father was out of work, we had to do with what we had. We had a cow and chickens, so we had milk and eggs."

"To this day, I don't like eggs. We had a garden, and my job was to pick the potato bugs off the vegetables. Then, I would put the bugs in a small can of kerosene to kill them."

Do you remember the end of the war?

"Yes, I do. I was seventeen years old in high school. My friends and I took my grandmother's aluminum wash tub and metal spoons, and we marched three or four blocks around the neighborhood. There were firecrackers, horns honking, and bells ringing."

How did WWII affect your life?

"I remember vividly the black-out drills we had during this time. There would be a siren, and then you had to pull the blinds and turn out all the lights. It would be dark because I don't recall any during the daytime. The neighborhood children and I played on our block, and we were near the end of the street. There was a German boy, Benny, who lived on our block. He rode his bike, and I held on to it with my roller skates on. He would go slowly, and when he started pedaling fast, I would let go and skate on my own. It was a good safe place to play. I never knew if anyone bullied him since he went to the Catholic school. I know at our school if someone wanted to bully someone, they would call them a 'kraut' or 'nazi.'"

"My mother and father separated and divorced when I was a sophomore in high school. I think there was a lot of stress on families. We moved to Columbus to live with my grandparents, and I went with my mother to seek a better climate for her health."

"In 1945, the doctor told my mother to leave the Indiana climate because she had lost a lot of weight and her heart was enlarged. She was not in good health at all. Her sister, my cousin, and I went with my mother to Albuquerque, New Mexico. However, my mother could not live there because of the high altitude which caused her to pass out. I enrolled in Albuquerque High School, but we were only there three months before I came back home to Indiana. I was in three high schools in four years. This was not unusual at this time, as families moved around trying to find jobs."

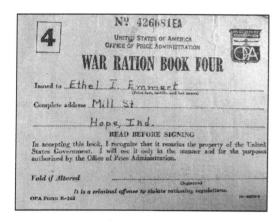

"We had to be careful and not waste anything. We had ration books with stamps that had to be accountable. Since we had a large family, our stamps were mostly all used up. I personally didn't go to the grocer, but my mother did. My husband's family had one child, so there were extra ration stamps left over in their book."

"When we lived in Columbus, the high school was smaller and many of the boys had quit school to join the military. I graduated from Columbus High School. I met my husband, William Emmert, or Bill, at the end of March 1946. After the life I had been through, I was ready to settle down and get married. He had been a radioman on a command ship in the Pacific battles – the Philippines, Okinawa, and Iwo Jima. Radio men took and received messages and sent them to the commander who alerted other ships."

What did you do for the war effort?

"Our English teacher encouraged the class to write to servicemen. I wrote to my older cousin who lived in Ohio and had joined the Air Force. I wrote about what we were doing and what the weather would be. I asked him questions about whether he was on the ground or flying a lot. He would write back and answer my questions."

"We saved rubber bands and the tin foil from sticks of chewing gum and rolled them in a ball. Also, we collected pennies for servicemen; we turned them in and things were bought and sent to them. The men would buy food or something to read. These were the things that we did for them."

What do you want America to know about your WWII experiences?

"I think the most important word in our language is patriotism. When you have patriotism, you have respect. I see people who don't have respect for other people. Parents teaching their children respect is very important. It's hard sometimes when you see all these things going on. I have never missed an election; I have always voted. I can't say I have always voted right, but I tried anyway."

"I wished I could have gone on to school, but we just lived day by day really. I have always been a reader, but it was more for escape. I love English history now. Yes, I probably could have done better by not marrying so soon and working my way through school. I could have gotten some type of training; however, at the time it seemed like the best thing to do. At my senior prom, my husband couldn't go; it was only for the students in that school. I went to the prom for two and half hours, and when I left, he was waiting for me. We went to a restaurant and got something to eat. On the night I graduated, I was asked to wear a diamond ring – we were engaged. We met on a blind date that my sister arranged."

What was your greatest achievement in your life?

"After the war was over in 1946, my husband, Bill, and I were married and raised four great children."

Bernice Groves

Bernice lived on a ranch near Gillette, Wyoming, during WWII. She was nine years old at the start of the war and remembered hearing about the bombing of Pearl Harbor on the radio. "My grandfather smoked a Bull Durham cigarette and listened to Edward R. Murrow every night. My uncle, John Ed New, was stationed aboard the USS *West Virginia* which was stationed at Pearl Harbor. He said that once they were hit, they jumped overboard and swam ashore. Everyone was quite worried because it took some time to notify the family of his safety. Thankfully, he was safe and uninjured."

What did you and your family do to help the war effort on the home front?

"My sister, Edra Drake, my dad, Ed Willard, and I collected scrap metal and old rubber tires that were not being used. Gillette was fifty miles away from where we lived. I think, we took it to be dropped off at a service station. I don't know how much we received from the sale of the tires and scrap metals, but we took the money to the post office to buy stamps for war bonds. It probably took six or eight weeks to collect enough stamps for a savings bond. The stamps would be placed in a book. When the book was completed, we exchanged it for a savings bond. The stamps for the book cost about twenty-five cents. The community of Gillette, Wyoming, collected silk hose for the war effort."

How did WWII affect your life?

"We had ration cards and never had any problems with them. We never ran out of anything. The soil in our area wasn't very good for a garden. We bought can goods by the case, then recycled the tin cans for the war effort. We went to Gillette once a week to check on my grandmother, so we didn't spend a lot of money on gas because we didn't go many places."

"My mother sewed many of our clothes, so that cut down on the expenses. I wore jeans to school, and there were only five children in the whole school. The next year there were only three children. Neighbors got together and helped each other do big chores like tagging the lambs. The nearest neighbor was three miles away. So, we didn't spend a lot of money going places."

What do you remember about WWII?

"We went to the movies once a week when we went to Gillette on Saturday. They always had a double feature, and it cost a dime. The movies began with a fifteen or twenty-minute newsreel about how the war was going. That made the biggest impression on me than anything else. I remember seeing the war pictures of Germany and Italy. Mostly it showed the concentration camps and the people on the trains."

"Everyone wanted to help, so many women got jobs to help the war effort. The nearest factories to me would have been in California. We got most of our war news from the radio. Everyone was happy when the war was finally over. Many of the neighbors' sons were in the military. A few of the guys were deferred because the United States needed them for farming and ranching."

Dolores Baker Herman

Irvin "Herm" Herman and Dolores Baker met on a blind date at the Rollerland skating rink, two days before she turned sixteen. Irvin, seventeen years old, had come to Indianapolis from Pennsylvania to Navy Radio School. Irvin wrote lots of letters to Dolores while he was overseas, and like all letters sent from war zones, they were reviewed by censors. When one of his letters arrived, Dolores found a note from the censor that said, 'I think he loves you.'

How did WWII affect your life?

"In 1941, I began high school at Shortridge High School at the beginning of the war and graduated in 1945. We were the only class that started in war and ended in war." Many famous people graduated from Shortridge High School in Indianapolis, Indiana, Former Indiana Senator Richard Lugar and famous author Kurt Vonnegut, for instance. Dolores has her high school yearbook and the first pages feature classmates who were in the service. "I didn't realize until later that many Jewish classmates attended Shortridge," Dolores said. "They were just kids like me."

Gas rationing ~

Dolores has kept a gas rationing book from the war times. "At that time, my dad's parents moved to Charlottesville, Indiana, a little town about thirty-five miles east of Indianapolis. My dad would save all our gas coupons for going out there."

"There were three books, one for each person in the home."

What was your greatest achievement in your life?

"The only thing I ever wanted to do was get married and have children. I never had big goals of being a nurse, a teacher or work in an office. My last semester of high school I only had classes in the morning. I got a job in the afternoon at Aetna Insurance. I took the streetcar downtown to my job. After I graduated, I worked there full time until we moved to Lafayette, so Irvin could complete his degree at Purdue University."

What are some events that you remember?

"Most of the boys were in the service when they graduated, some of them before they graduated. To have a date, you had to meet a serviceman, and I met a lot of the young men. I had a good time, even after Herm was overseas. I didn't say, 'I'll wait for you;' because I still had two years of high school left." Dolores kept some military patches from some servicemen whom she knew during the war.

Do you remember the beginning of WWII?

"It was on a Sunday, and I remember listening to it on the radio when we found out about the attack on Pearl Harbor."

What do you want America to know about your experiences?

"It certainly is different in how we get our news now. We would have to go to the movies to see battles that happened two weeks before. Everything was delayed. That's why in one of our high school classes, we had a big map of the world. We would use pushpins, after we read in the newspapers where our troops were located. We would put a pin on the map where the battle was being fought. I guess this helped us to keep things as up to date as anything else."

"We also had paper drives and collected tin cans to recycle. Being brought up during the Depression, we didn't have that much extra stuff. So, we never missed a lot of things. I thought I was very deprived because I never had twenty-five cents to go to the high school basketball game. I thought that was awful. The scores were like twelve and nine, so it wasn't much of a game. We just knew we couldn't have certain things. We never missed it because we never had it."

After the war~

"My brother, Wayne, had two fingers cut off in an accident while working. The military would not take him into the service, and he was ridiculed because of this. However, when the war was over, Wayne was drafted and went to Germany."

When the war ended, Irvin returned to Indianapolis and the couple were married In August 1946. Irvin and Dolores have been married more than seventy years.

Dolores and Irwin

Janet Holderness

"I grew up in the hills of Hollywood, California in the thirties and forties. It was only one block, called a blind street, which made it ideal for my brothers and me to play. Ronald Colman, the actor, had a tennis court which drew many film stars like Ginger Rogers in her blue convertible. Other actors like David Niven and Adolph Menjou would stop and play ball with us. Janet Gaynor built an amazing park next to her house which made it ideal for Hide and Seek."

"When I turned seventeen, my mother took me to visit relatives on the East Coast. This was the turning point in my life. We stayed with the Commandant of Cadets who invited a cadet for dinner and the Hop. I fell in love right then! World War Two broke out a few months later. In the summer of 1942, my cadet was able to choose a base by my home to learn basic flying, so we had time to get to know each other."

"A year later, in June 1943, he graduated from West Point, and I was able to secure a train ticket to join him. Soon he was sent to England to prepare for the Invasion. In 1944, his unit was flying all over France and Germany supporting General Patton. During this time, we kept track of each other by numbered letters which I have saved in four shoe boxes. This is a way nobody does anymore, but it is a valuable keepsake. These are true treasures. Finally, he returned from the war, and I had just graduated from Berkeley, so the time had finally come to be married. This was the beginning of twenty-six moves in the military!"

"When stationed in England I would organize get-togethers with local housewives in their villages to understand the Air Force missions. Many of them were terrified by the noisy bombers. Memories still linger, and I still write to several of them today. We even created a small polo team to play with the British. I am very proud that we received the American Ambassador's award for community relations that year. Another time when we lived in Denver, Colorado, I enjoyed visiting local colleges to meet young ladies and prepare them to understand the role of a service wife. This was in the early formative years of the new Air Force Academy before it was established in Colorado Springs. The first class graduated in 1959, and I was thrilled to see some of my ladies now preparing to marry their cadet. These are a few of my adventures as an Air Force wife."

Jan and Bud Holderness

Johnson, Betty Bee

Betty attended Butler University in Indianapolis for two years. In 1940, soon after college, Betty married Dick Johnson. One story Betty relates is about the time she and her sister Pat were driving to Ft. Sibert, Alabama, to see their husbands who were in the military. "Sometimes I would nurse the baby while I was driving. Well, I didn't want to stop. We had a flat tire about midnight. I walked down the hill to a tavern, where a man said he would help us. He fixed our flat tire, and we were on our way again."

Do you remember what you were doing when the war was over?

"No, I don't. We were just so excited." Betty has a picture of downtown Indianapolis during the end of the war in Europe. The caption in the Indianapolis newspaper states, "Lights went on again for half the world as Hitler's Fortress Europe fell. Here is Indianapolis' share. For the first time in many months show windows, electric signs, and theater marquees were alight, almost blinding in the unaccustomed intensity. The blaze of light was a symbol of victory and a warning to Japan that we can whip her and have lights, too."

How did WWII affect your life?

"It made me more independent. It was very trying, and when he (Betty's husband) left, he wanted me to stay in the house, so he would have a place to come back to. I was expecting our first child at any minute. Dick was drafted in March 1943, and the baby was due in April. My folks lived around the corner, and my sister Emily lived with me. Dick came home from the military in December 1945."

What was a funny or unexpected event?

"My sister Emily had a husband who was stationed at Ft. Knox, Kentucky. At the time, she was living with me. When she came home from work, she turned on the water heater to take a bath. We had steam heat in the double we lived in. When she came in, she always rushed, and forgot to turn the water heater off. About two o'clock that morning, I went to the bathroom and when I flushed the toilet, it exploded! Since it was steam heat, the heat must have built up, and it exploded. Parts of the kitchen ceiling fell onto my cabinets. I wasn't hurt, but I rushed to my bedroom window and yelled, 'help.' The fellow across the street was just getting home from night work, and he and his buddy came over. The fellow next door came over. I was a nervous wreck. My daughter, Bunny, was about a year old. I thought what if she had been in her walker in this area during the explosion. It was a very trying time."

What did you do for the war effort?

"I had two years training at Butler University when Dick went into the service. Dick's father said he would help me set up a kindergarten in my house. In 1944-45, I turned my dining room into a kindergarten room. We took up the rug and put down Mother Goose linoleum, and I had small tables and chairs. I had a good group of fourteen or fifteen children. Several of the children had fathers who were in the service. I received thirty dollars a month for each of the children."

"Also, I had quite a few ladies whose husbands were in the service and would come over to my house for dinner. I made angel food cake from scratch and cooked hamburgers. Hamburger was ten cents a pound. We had our cries, but I tried to cheer them up and become their confidant. My sisters-in-laws had husbands in the service, and we would build each other up. I was the oldest of five children."

"My sister Pat's husband, Fred, was in Patton's army and sent overseas. Fred was killed when he reached the top of the hill; supposedly, he was killed by friendly fire by one of his own men, perhaps because the men didn't like him. He was a red head and had a temper. He had a heart of gold, but a quick temper."

How did the rationing affect you?

"We had sugar and gas rationing which was the hardest. I finally gave up the car and had to share rides with my family. That's the only way we could get around. We lived across the street from the grocery, and the owner would let us charge our groceries. We would pay when our money came in. People ate as little as they could; plus, they ate a lot of bread and potatoes."

What do you think was your greatest achievement?

"Independence, being able to take care of the family while my husband was away. You had to, as the furnaces required you to build fires and carry out the ashes. It either built you up or tore you down – one or the other. We really had to become independent." Her motto is to be positive.

What do you want America to know about your experiences during WWII?

"I think it makes you more independent and thoughtful of other people. Everybody worked together. During that time, people learned to do without and didn't grumble about it. We were all for our men and women to come home safely and soon. We learned sharing, giving, patience, helping each other, and believing in and respecting our country. Our flag said everything we believed. After the war, people had greater respect for each other - faith and trust in God, each other, and our America!"

Maxine Jones

How did WWII affect your life?

"I was very upset when my husband, Dan, left for the service. I had my daughter, Rita, who was eleven months old, so I moved in with my parents. My parents lived in Oatville on a farm in Gibson County, north of Princeton, Indiana. You didn't just jump in the car and go somewhere for the fun of it because gasoline and tires were rationed. We had plenty to eat because of the farm, and we had ration stamps for additional food. I had one girlfriend who lived close to my parents, but back then my dad didn't allow any running around for a married lady. So, there wasn't much to do. You didn't miss all these things we do today because we never had them. We had a little town with a couple grocery stores, a one room school, a blacksmith shop, a feed store, and a church. Outside of church on Wednesday night and church on Sunday, there were no activities."

Do you remember the beginning of the war?

"I had a brother, Buel Hunt, who was in the war; He was drafted into the Army 38th Division. We didn't know when he was going to come back home. However, he did come home safely. Dan had a brother and cousin in the war. My cousin, Earl Lewis, lost a leg in combat."

"In October 1943, Dan was drafted into the Marines and stationed at Camp Pendleton in San Diego, California. I took two trips by train to see him. You didn't get on an airplane in those days. On one trip I took my mother and Rita with me. Rita developed measles on the train, and she cried all the time. The servicemen on the train would walk and carry her around to make her feel better. The civilians were supposed to give up their seats to the servicemen, but we didn't have to do it this time. At the dining cars, the servicemen got to go before the civilians."

"The only men who were around our town were young boys and old men. You didn't see men of draft age; they were all gone."

Dan and the Indiana guys - photo taken by Ernie Pyle

"Dan was in Okinawa as well as China during his time in the service. He has a picture of a group of guys and him looking at the Japanese flag. The photo was taken by Ernie Pyle, an Indiana native and famous war correspondent of WWII. Dan said, 'All the guys in the picture were from Indiana.'" Dan met Ernie and talked with him. Ernie Pyle lived in Dana, Indiana, about eighty miles west of Indianapolis. Pyle was killed by the Japanese in 1945 and was buried at the Punchbowl Cemetery in Hawaii.

Do you remember the end of the war?

"When the war was over, I got excited thinking we would all  be together. However, the Marines sent Dan to China for about three or four months, before he was able to come home." Dan's group was sent to China to disarm the Japanese at the end of the war. He came home on the USS *Wakefield*.

Homecoming~

"He came home on Valentine's Day 1946. I went to pick him up at Princeton, Indiana, during a horrible snowstorm." Dan said, "I had to wait for a certain train that stopped in Princeton from Chicago."

"My grandfather had a little three-room house out in the country that I fixed up for us when Dan returned. So, I had our furniture in it and ready for his return. We were able to have some private time. Rita picked up his picture and talked to it while he was gone. Dan weighed a hundred thirty-four pounds when he returned. When he got off the train with his heavy coat on, he looked different with the weight he had gained. We had not seen him for about a year and a half."

What was your greatest achievement in your life?

"Having four children – two boys and two girls."

What do you want America to know about your experiences?

"I am just so thankful that I got him back; That would be my message to America."

Dan Jones

Did you have any regrets about this time in your life?

"I had a lot to be thankful for. I had parents who welcomed my child and me back home to live with them. I didn't think the Army would draft Dan since he had a wife and child. However, he was drafted and didn't come home until he was discharged."

Millicent "Millie" Lemen

"In 1941, I was ten years old when the war started. Our schools were very patriotic, and we sang service songs for each branch of the military. In geography class, we had a map and the teacher showed us where some of the battles were located. We were very limited to where we could go and what we could do, so I rode my bike to most places. As kids we played war games; we became the Americans and the Germans instead of cowboys and Indians. We were into the war; sometimes I got my dad's WWI uniform and wore it."

How did WWII affect your life?

"It didn't affect my life too much. Everything was done for me. I was the youngest of four girls in my family. We had ration books, and mother would take care of all the cooking and shopping for food. Meat, coffee, and gasoline were rationed. The things I can remember most are what went on at school. We had grease collections. Whenever mother would cook and have grease leftover, we would put it in a can. When the can was full, I would take it to school where it was collected in a barrel at the back of the schoolyard. I believe it was used in making armaments."

"We collected newspapers all the time too. About once a month Victory Bonds would be sold. For eighteen dollars and seventy-five cents, you could buy a bond, and when it matured, you would get twenty-five dollars for it. We saved up stamps as kids, then traded them in for a bond. Also, I

sold newspapers on the corner of Arlington Avenue and Washington Street with the boy down the street. On the day President Roosevelt died, I sold extra papers on this street corner. When the war was over on V-E Day and V-J Day, I sold papers there too."

Millie and Specky

"Gasoline was rationed, so that limited vacations. My dad, Charles Eugene Lemen, was called Gene, and worked for Stokely-Van Camp in Indianapolis. We had plenty of can goods, since he brought home the dented cans and the ones with no labels. He was so busy working at the company that we didn't see much of him. His job was to get the C-Rations for the troops packaged and loaded on trains. I remember him talking about the number of train cars that they had to load with C-Rations. He brought some of them home for us to sample. He had a top priority job because of the military contract for the C-Rations. He got extra gas ration stamps so that he could go to his job."

"When we went on vacation to Wisconsin, stores would not sell meat to us. They saved it to sell to the locals. We were able to get some bear meat though. It was not very good as it had a wild taste to it. We were able to get by with some fish to eat."

What did you do for the war effort?

"Toward the end of the war, I rode the bus downtown to roll bandages for the Red Cross. By 1945, I was probably fourteen years old and able to ride the bus alone. Many people donated blood plasma for the war." People were helping the war effort in many ways.

What was the greatest achievement in your life?

"I was the only one in my family that went to college. After I graduated from Hanover College, I received my degree. I lived in Terre Haute, Indiana, teaching at Indiana State University for many years."

What do you remember about the end of the war?

"There was a big to-do downtown on Monument Circle. I tried to go, but my parents would not let me. My older sister, Dorothy, went to the celebration though. People were in the fountains and all the servicemen that were around were kissing the girls. Celebrations like this occurred in many other places in America."

Did you feel like a regular child, or teenager, during this time?

Millie felt like she was a regular child during the war. Like many other children of the 1940's, she went to the movies on Saturday. "I remember going to the movie every week, and they had a short newsreel at the beginning of the movie. They showed a lot of the battle scenes of the war. So many kids had relatives in the military. There was a cartoon and a serial every week; sometimes the serial would be someone lying on the railroad tracks or other dangerous situations." She remembered seeing *Gone With The Wind* but didn't have a favorite movie.

Did you think about the war very much?

"We knew how it was going to end. We knew who was going to come out on top. There was no question. We knew what was going on, but we may not have known how bad it was or what life was like for the troops. Life went on as usual for us. Our family took at least two of the three newspapers that were printed in Indianapolis. So, we knew what was happening in the war."

Mildred "Millie" Mahurin

How did WWII affect your life?

"Prior to WWII women stayed home and took care of the family; when the war began in Europe in 1939, life began to change. When the United States entered the war in 1941, a lot of the men left for the war or were drafted. The economy was better during the war."

Left to right – Millie, her sister, Marthajean and unidentified girl.

Rationing during the war ~

"Ration books – eggs, flour, coffee and sugar, you would have to have the coupons. Inside the ration books were small coupons that you would tear off when you bought something at the store. People borrowed a cup of sugar or flour. That's what neighbors did back then. You don't see much of that today. I saw the Omar and Wonder bread men and milk trucks who delivered in our neighborhood. The milk company would let the bill go for a while because they knew it was difficult for a single mom to support five kids alone. I remember our family getting milk, but not bread. The smell of bread baking was wonderful. We lived near the bakery at 13th and Bellefontaine Ave."

The Omar Bakery, in operation during the 1930's and 1940's in Indianapolis, Indiana, is still standing at 16th Street bought by Continental Baking Company and Omar Bakery ceased operation by 1966. (Indianapolis Star, March 11, 2018)

"At school, we were taught to respect the flag. In art, we made flyers that pertained to the war. I made an airplane and wrote these words, 'keep 'em flying.' We hung them in the classroom. I don't remember writing letters, but my mom wrote to my uncle who was in the service. In school, we didn't write letters to the military men, but we respected the military. We were all concerned about the war and our country. We were very patriotic and obeyed the rules of the land. Parents as well as teachers taught the children about the war. We were all involved in it and prayed for the soldiers."

"In the window of houses there were religious sayings about praying for the soldiers. My uncle, my mother's brother, Paul Esch, was a cook and would sneak food out for the children in France. He would give food to the local people. He would come home and tell about the dead bodies he saw. We all cried when he told us about the deaths."

"There were no McDonalds or fast food places to eat, except White Castle; we ate at home. We had a lot of potatoes and beans. Mom could make three meals out of one chicken. Mom was a good cook, and everybody loved her cooking. My mother wanted everything to look pretty, even though we were poor. Everybody in the family ate at the same time; we didn't eat anything before meals. There were three meals a day before she separated from my father. When he wouldn't work, she left him and got a job as a cook in a restaurant. She would prepare meals before she went to work in the evening. She gave my sister and me orders on what to do while she was gone. When I was thirteen or fourteen, I cleaned houses and babysat to earn money. When I was sixteen, I worked about twenty or twenty-five hours a week and earned eighteen dollars. I gave most of it to my mother."

What do you want American to know about your experiences?

"We were proud of our country and our military and loyal to the military and respected them. This was taught in school and at home."

What did your family do for the war effort?

"We didn't have plastic or aluminum foil. We saved gum wrappers and made a little ball of them. I don't remember how we sent it on to be recycled. There weren't plastic bags for the trash cans like we have today. I remember mom saving everything, as it was recycled for the war. We saved scrap metal and had a scrap drive. Anybody that had scrap metal, a broken bicycle or car pieces, wheeled it in their wagon to the scrapyard. We got a few pennies or fifteen or twenty cents for it depending on how much we had. They weighed it and paid you for whatever amount you would have."

"We had to smash our corn and green bean cans and save them and our bacon grease for the war use. They used these things for the war, and it was picked up once a month by the city. We saved any kind of paper, and we had paper sales at school. Whoever brought the most papers to school got a prize about every three months."

What was your greatest achievement in your life?

"My greatest achievement was becoming a mother. In September 1949, I married my husband, Melvin, when I was eighteen. I was not career minded because at that time most women got married and had children. I raised six children; two are gone now. I was proud to become a mom. I didn't go to work; I stayed home: baked, cooked, and sewed the children's clothes."

What was your greatest regret about this time?

"I had to quit school to help my mom with the bills. In 1944-45, my family lived on Arch Street, and the rent was twelve dollars and fifty cents a month. I remember walking to the rental company to pay the rent; I was about thirteen years old. The lady there reminded me that the rent was late. She didn't need to remind me; I paid the bills."

"I didn't finish high school with my class and have always regretted it. In 1974, I finished high school and went on to Ivy Tech. Then my husband got sick, and I quit school to take care of him. I am still learning and have never quit learning, and always wanted to be a teacher. I am what God made me to be, and I am satisfied with it."

Millie's Eighth Grade Class

Louise May

How did WWII affect your life?

"I was sixteen years old when the war began in 1941. Fort Harrison was starting a finance office. The government was doing this all over the states at this time. So, they needed someone to take care of the officers' pay and things like that. Someone at Fort Harrison called the principal at my high school and asked him if there was anyone graduating they could use. I had been very close to the principal and the teachers during my last two years of school. It was a very small school that had all the grades together. There were about twenty-five seniors in my graduating class. In 1943, the principal of my school, Lawrence High School, recommended me."

"There were some barracks that were converted into offices, and I was in charge of paying the officers. Some of them had been injured, and I was to pay them their monthly wage. I went there not knowing much, but I paid the officers when they came in from a trip."

"I wanted to attend college, but my father said I didn't need to go. My father had not gone to college, and that was the thinking at the time. Now we think differently. I liked drawing and wanted to increase my knowledge about art, and I wanted to be an art teacher. I got good grades and liked going to school. There were four children in the family, and I was the second oldest child."

"Some of the officers that were able to walk around came up to the offices for their pay. They were always kidding me and talking. They would include me; it was fun, and I enjoyed meeting all the officers. They were jolly even after all the things they had seen."

What do you remember about when the war was over?

"Oh my, yes. When Ft. Harrison announced the war was over, they closed everything at Ft. Harrison. In front of the main building and office, on both sides of the street, they put up long tables. The people in charge of the Finance Center served a delicious dinner for us all. There were a lot of stories going around and laughing and fun things. One of the tall guys grabbed me and put me up on his shoulders. He said, 'look everybody, I'm taking her home to my mom. I think she will approve. What do you think?' Then he ran me up the steps to the main office and around the back of the building. When he came down, everyone was clapping. It was fun and quite a celebration."

"I worked at the Finance Center until the war was over. All the civilians were let go when the war was over. I found another job for three days; then, Fort Harrison asked me to come back and take care of Billings Hospital. They wanted me to take care of the money like I did before the war was over. So, that is what I did. Ft. Harrison built a small hospital by putting together several barracks. There was about five or six of us to take care of the finances."

What is your greatest regret about this time of your life?

"I have no regrets; I have been very lucky. I didn't have to go around looking for a job. I learned a lot in a short time."

What do you want America to know about your experiences?

"I just worked with the officers and paid them their travel money. They were all just fine men. I never met one that was not very courteous and very good. I wish I could hear how they are doing now. The officers didn't talk about the war and what they had been doing. Sometimes I had to pay the officers that were still unable to walk. My boss at the Finance Office told me if some of the officers want to talk to you, 'just stay there and talk.' It didn't matter how long I stayed. They talked about their family; it was too hard to talk about things that they had seen. I didn't hear a whole about the war; I just listened to what they wanted to talk about."

What was your greatest achievement in your life?

"My children were the greatest achievement in my life. After the war, I met my husband when our family went to Lake Barbee in northern Indiana. My dad liked to fish, and we stayed in a cabin along the lake. Robert, my future husband, had just come home from the Navy. His family wanted to give him a vacation before he finished college. We were staying in cabins next to each other on Lake Barbee."

Louise and Robert at Lake Barbee

"When I got out of the car, I saw this tall guy walking along the lake. I said, 'Ooh, who's that?' They said, 'It's the boy next door.' That evening, there was a boat tour of the lake. So, the two of us, the four younger children, and my cousin went on the tour. When we got back, the younger children said, 'We saw everything, but Louise and our brother, Robert, didn't see anything because they just sat and talked.' We started dating, and I was twenty-one years old at the time. I told him that we had to wait until he was twenty-one. We got married in November 1947, a week before his had five children and a busy family."

Louise on her wedding day

Mary Plummer

Do you remember when the war began?

"I remember when Pearl Harbor was attacked in December 1941. Dad had the radio on, and he heard it. We were all very astounded and horrified at the bombing. It was unsettling that it had happened. My parents were especially upset about it."

"In 1944, we lived in Indianapolis, Indiana, and I went to Tech High School. Dad's brother and his wife lived in San Diego, California. They said to come out to California, as there were a lot of jobs available because of the war. We sold our house and probably kept too many things for the camper. My family left Indianapolis and started to California in our car and a loaded down camper. We blew so many tires that we stopped in Odon, Indiana, to visit aunts and uncles for a while." Odon is about ninety miles southwest of Indianapolis. "We ended up staying in Odon for about six months and then returning to Indianapolis. We never did make it to California."

"Odon was a small town and very enjoyable. They had a teen canteen where young people could go to meet each other. The teen canteen had a juke box and a nice place to go. The town had a drugstore and a movie theater. It was a different type of life than what we had in Indianapolis."

How did WWII affect your life?

"In 1944, my brother, Paul, was older when he graduated and joined the Navy. That affected our lives a lot; however, he didn't see any combat and didn't go overseas. We got our war news from the radio and listened to the newsreels at the movies; it was informative about the war."

What did your family do for the war effort?

"While we were living in Odon, Indiana, my mom got a job at Crane – Naval Ammunition Depot. Mom had secretarial skills but didn't drive a car. There were people with whom she could get a ride to work with though. She worked as a secretary at Crane Naval Depot. According to the U.S. Army website, www.army.mil, "The base originally was established as a naval ammunition depot in December 1941 on the eve of WWII with the mission of producing and shipping munitions to the fleet.""

Do you remember when WWII ended?

"I remember the celebration in Odon, Indiana, on V-E Day." V-E Day, the victory in Europe during May 1945, is designated as the day the Allies of World War II accepted the surrender of Nazi Germany. "People were honking their car horns because they were so happy. I didn't go downtown and was about fifteen years old. It was a good time and the United States was celebrating."

Do you have any regrets about your experiences during this time?

"I may have had some regrets about leaving my home in Indianapolis and moving to Odon, but it was such a good experience with everyone being so nice. I don't have any regrets. I got acquainted with other teens, and it was a different experience than I would have had in Indianapolis."

What do you want America to know about your experiences?

"I do think there were a lot of people in Odon and Indianapolis who were very patriotic and did things that would help the country. My husband was stationed in Manila. When the United States dropped the atomic bomb on Hiroshima, my husband and some friends had gone to a movie. They interrupted the movie to tell them what had happened. The guys didn't know what an atomic bomb was. However, there was one guy who took science in school and knew what an atomic reaction was."

What was your greatest achievement in your life?

"In November 1947, Harold and I were married. So, my sixty-one year marriage and my four daughters were my greatest achievement."

Sue Stockwell

How did WWII affect your life?

"Probably, not a lot. I lived in rural Owen county, Indiana,

with my grandmother, Nellie, and my aunt, Marjorie. I didn't live with my father, who lived in Indianapolis, because my mother died of cancer before I started school. It was a peaceful time, and my friends and I would spend many summer days at Lake Hollybrook near where we lived."

"My life changed when my aunt Marjorie married and moved to Illinois. In 1942, I left Gosport and went to live with my dad, who had remarried when I was fourteen. During my freshman year of high school, I attended Shortridge High School. Everything was rationed, especially food items and gas. My dad drove a very old Plymouth that belonged to his dad. You couldn't buy a new car during this time. "My dad, Charles Thompson, worked for Marmon Herrington which made military vehicles and tanks during the war." According to the website, www.usautoindustry.com, the company made various tanks and armored trucks that were fitted with armor and armament which the military used in South Africa. Marmon Herrington built tanks for the U. S. Marines and the U.S. Army.

"I wasn't too much aware of the war while living in Gosport, in Owen county, about fifty miles southwest of Indianapolis; however, once I moved to Indianapolis I was aware of all the servicemen. There were a lot of soldiers from Fort Harrison and sailors from the Naval Academy on the White River. Girls didn't go around by themselves because of all the servicemen. We went in groups because the servicemen were standing around on street corners; that's what you did. If you went into a restaurant by yourself, it wouldn't be any time before a serviceman would be over introducing himself. I met and dated some of them; usually, I knew them before they went into the service. That's how I met my husband, Bill."

How did you meet your husband?

"I worked part time during my junior and senior year in high school at John Hancock Insurance Company in the Circle Tower building. If you had good enough grades and the course work, you could skip lunch and study hall. So, I agreed to go to work in the afternoons. From Shortridge High School, I had to take a streetcar to get downtown Indianapolis. After graduation, I worked at John Hancock full time."

"About once a week, five or six of us girls would get together

 after work and go get something to eat and go to a movie. We liked to go to Wheelers restaurant nearby. We walked up there because the restaurant was known for waffles. On one occasion, there was a group of five or six guys that came into the restaurant. The guys weren't in uniform, but they started talking to us, and Bill was one of the guys. We exchanged phone numbers, but he didn't call me, so I thought, 'He's not going to call me.'"

"One day on my lunch hour, I walked out the door of the Circle Tower building, and 'Who should I run into'? - Bill Stockwell. This was January 5, 1946, after he was discharged from the service. On Thanksgiving Day, November 28, 1946, we were married, and it snowed like crazy."

What was your greatest achievement in your life?

"My greatest achievement was my family. I grew up as an only child, and I had one daughter after three years of marriage. Then it was about nine years before I became pregnant with my second daughter. Also, I had a good marriage."

What do you want America to know about your experiences?

"It was a bad time for my husband, but it turned out to be good for me after the war experience. It makes you appreciate the good things rather than the war stories that went on. Bill did not talk a lot about his war experiences, unless we had friends in to visit who had been in the war. Then the guys would talk about their war experiences on Iwo Jima. Bill was in the infantry on Iwo Jima for forty-six days and during that time his helmet was half full of water. That amount of water was all he had to wash his face in while he was there. He was wounded but not seriously."

Do you have any regrets about this time?

"I always wanted to be a school teacher. My aunt Marjorie was a teacher, and I regret I didn't have the opportunity to attend college and become a teacher; however, I have a daughter that is a teacher."

What did you do for the war effort?

"I wrote letters to the servicemen that I knew or met. I knew Harold Hancock when I lived in Gosport, Indiana. When he went into the service, I started writing to him. Harold gave me a small group of perforated stamps with my picture on them. I just tore off one of the stamps and licked the back to affix it to the corner of the letter. I guess it was to let him know which girl was writing to him."

"His parents lived in the Panama Canal Zone, but his aunt lived in Gosport near me. So, that is how we knew each other, and he had an aunt and uncle who lived in Indianapolis. When I moved to Indianapolis, we remained in contact with each other. When we were sixteen or seventeen, we dated and continued to still stay in touch while he was in the service."

"My girlfriends and I went to the movies and saw the newsreels about the war. The speaker on the newsreels was Lowell Thomas. I always thought they were very interesting, and it brought the war home when you saw the killing and devastation. There were the homeless people which made you more aware of what was going on in the war. We went to the Circle Theater or the Loews Theater. My girlfriends and I went to see Frank Sinatra and Tommy Dorsey in concert at the Circle Theater." The Indiana Theater is on Washington Street in downtown Indianapolis. Today, it is a beautifully restored theater in the heart of Indianapolis. "I went to some dances at the Indiana Ballroom and there were many servicemen. There was always a lot of good music and dancers."

Bula Walton

Victor and Bula were married in 1938 in a small ceremony at a parsonage in southeastern Indiana. They had six children, five girls and one boy, and were married over sixty years before Victor's death in 1996.

What do you remember about the beginning of the war?

"We heard it on the radio. We had a good radio, so we got all the good news and the bad news too. We listened every day to see if anyone we knew was hurt or killed. It wasn't a pleasant time, but it was what you made it."

How did WWII affect your life?

"Well, for one thing it took my husband away for a year. We had two little girls and another child that was born while he was gone. My husband, Victor, was in the Army and on the first ship that went into Japan. In 1945, it was a sad time when he had to leave for the service. He had nothing but nice things to say about the Japanese people. The Japanese people helped the soldiers as much as they could. We didn't know what the military would face when they walked into Japan."

"I don't have many pleasant memories of WWII really. It wasn't that bad either because we had plenty to eat, so we didn't have to worry about that. I lived in the country and had an old Model A Ford which I drove into town to pick up our groceries. My kids didn't know what a kid's car seat was in those days."

"We lost a lot of people in the war; it wasn't a pleasant time, but it wasn't an impossible time either. We had six family members that were in WWII. I think most people can adjust to hard times if they want to. I had one baby while my husband was gone, but it wasn't that bad."

"I wrote letters to Victor every day about what the children were doing. The letters didn't catch up with him for two or three months. I wrote a page to him every night. Victor didn't write much; maybe once a month I would get a letter from him. His letters were always welcome."

How did you deal with the rationing during this time?

"Sugar and coffee were rationed. I didn't drink coffee so this wasn't a problem. I haven't really been a coffee drinker. I think you deal with what you have. To get sugar you had little stamps to take to the store to get a pound of sugar. To me, this was the one thing I missed the most because I always baked a lot. We didn't lose any weight, so I don't think it hurt us. My father stayed with us for a while, and he was a gardener. I canned food, so we had plenty to eat."

What do you want America to know about your experiences?

"I was lucky that I didn't lose anybody. Some of our family were in the Battle of the Bulge; one of them was my brother-in-law. I would change some things if I lived my life over; I might straighten out some things. Patience – with one another. If you lose your temper every time something happens, that's not good. I remember what my dad said when we were gathered around listening to the radio when Franklin D. Roosevelt was elected. He looked back at two or three of his sons and said, 'Get your guns ready, boys, you are going to be leaving'; It came true that we were in war soon."

What was your greatest achievement in your life?

"I have raised six kids, and they have all have turned out well. It's a blessing as I have fifteen grandchildren and thirty great-grandchildren."

What do you remember about the end of the war?

"My husband came home rather quickly after the war ended. He pulled up in a taxi into our yard. That was something! The girls were brand new, two and four years old, and some of the family were here to help welcome him home too. They were very excited about him coming home."

Bula has seen many changes in transportation in her century of life. "I went from a horse and buggy to an airplane. I enjoyed the horse and buggy more than the plane." She recalled traveling by horse and buggy with her parents from Wiesburg to Sunman, Indiana. Her family would ride the local train from one town to another when Bula was about six or seven years old. "I have seen a lot of changes in my life." Bula's motto in life is "Just hold on; this too will pass in life. I am still living that way."

Bula and Victor's anniversary

Author's Note~

Bula celebrated her 100th birthday on May 5, 2018; however, after a brief illness she passed away on August 17, 2018.

Letters from home ~

To keep the morale up for the soldiers who were far from home, often in a foreign country, the women of America wrote letters to relatives, friends, husbands or boyfriends. As one of the women who was interviewed replied, "If you didn't write, you were wrong." Women felt like it was another way that they could help with the war effort.

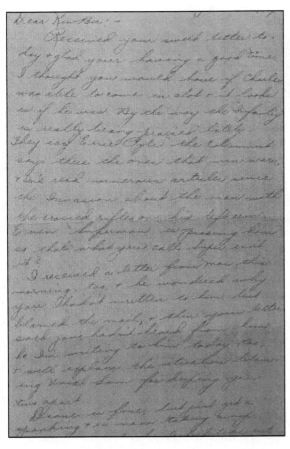

Several letters mentioned the D-day Invasion. D-Day, the Allied invasion of Normandy, began on June 6, 1944, in Normandy, France. It was also called Operation Overlord. Since the Axis powers were not aware of the exact location and time of the attack, it was a victory for the Allies, but not without massive loss of life on both sides. The Allied invasion was led by General Dwight Eisenhower who later became the thirty-fourth president of the United States.

June 20, 1944 letter from Virginia Minton to her sister, Miss Kew Bee McGregor

War news in the letter includes what the columnist Ernie Pyle had to say about who was winning the war. Kew Bee was in Oklahoma visiting her husband, Charles, who was in the Army Infantry. Virginia writes about the Invasion, which was the D-Day invasion of 1944. Mac is their brother who has not heard from Kew Bee for a while. Mac was in the Army Air Force in China.

Top row: Perry, Anna, Virginia, C Ray, Mary Jane, Art
Bottom row: Kew Bee, Charlie

Betty Slentz Poole

Betty wrote in her letter to husband, Bob, about the impending D-Day Invasion. An excerpt of Betty's letter to Bob dated May 21, 1944, is as follows:

> "Everyone is terribly anxious these days, awaiting D-Day. We all seem to be in a tension and keep our ears on the radio constantly for news of the great day. I do hope it comes soon and ends soon – for I know it will be a great loss of life. I'm so very thankful that you aren't in that area now, Rip (a nickname for Bob)." Bob was stationed in Tampa, Florida, at this time.

> "It is being stressed that there must be a great day of prayer on D-Day, for our boys and for our country, so the church will be opened all day on that day, and the church bell will ring several times during the day to let the people know the church is open. Then that evening there will be a prayer meeting."

Betty Slentz Poole wrote on June 6, 1944, the following letter to her husband, Bob (Rip).

> "It's D-Day, and my first and main thought all day long has been to thank God that my husband is not in the invasion forces. Do you suppose that's a selfish prayer, Rip? Wish you were here, so I could talk over with you all the thoughts that have been running through my mind, and hear yours, too. Mrs. Strong woke us at 6:00 A.M. to tell us the news, so I immediately hopped up and listened to all the news until 7:45, when I left the house. Of course, you know all the happenings, so I won't retell those, - only tell you my reactions."

"The church has been open all day, so I stopped there before going to the office, for prayer and to read my Bible. There was no one else there at the time, and I felt so very close to God. When I went in, I was feeling very depressed, but as I came out and saw the early morning sun, the flowers, the trees, the blue sky, and heard the birds singing, I felt that things weren't too bad – I felt safe, had a home, food and you were safe. I thought of those poor people in France and Germany – even though they (Germany) are our enemies, my heart aches for the women and children – their homes being destroyed, and many of the little children to die so innocently."

D-Day was a day for patriotism and optimism for the end of war to be near after so many years of killing and struggle.

"But it's a job that must be done, and there is surely a reason or I'm sure God would never have permitted it. I've just taken time out while President Roosevelt led the nation in prayer, and now they're singing "Onward, Christian Soldiers." It's a very wonderful thing for him to take time out to lead the prayer, and I'm sure that as a Christian nation we will win the victory. It seems as though our country – as a whole, was never before so united in prayer and faith in God – it makes us all feel so close and pulling together."

D-Day, however, was not a thankful day for those women whose loved ones were in harm's way. Betty wrote of two ladies whose husbands were in the combat areas during the fighting.

"My heart ached so, as I sat next to Betty Fulton and in front of Audrey McCartney. Betty's husband, you know

Is in England and Audrey's is a paratrooper, and was probably one of the first to land. They were both taking it pretty hard, and I tried to put myself in their places and imagine that you were there. Then I thanked God again that you were still here. It's been a great day in the history of our country, Rip..."

Love Letters Help Ease the Loneliness

Bob and Betty Poole were married for sixty-five years. Bob

was in the Army Air Corps and spent time in Japan after Japan surrendered. Betty wrote over five hundred letters to Bob during his military career. She wrote to Bob every day and sometimes included a secret message under the stamp. The message might be a favorite song title or quote. Some of the letters mentioned their wedding and future plans when the war was over.

Bob and Betty Poole letters

Rationing of hosiery

Many items were rationed, as several of the women have mentioned, and women had to adapt to new types of materials for their socks or hose. Betty Slentz Poole explained how difficult it was to find hose in her letter of January 3, 1946.

"I feel so rich tonight – at last I have two pair of hose – rayon, still – but they are hose! Do you know that for the past month the hosiery counters all over town have been completely bare? They've stopped making rayon – are just making a few nylons – so just once in a great while nylons come to the counters, and they sell out in a minute – of course, we poor working girls are never around to get any. Last week, I went to every store in town and all they had were cotton hose and black rayon – I just had to lean on the counter and laugh!"

"I got these two pairs through Ruth – she works at the Hosiery Mills, you know! I'd just have to quit going to work if it weren't for Ruth, for I was completely out. Nylons are supposed to be more plentiful in a few weeks – so here's hoping."

As the tide was turning for the Allies the home front was soon going to have to cope with returning soldiers. These soldiers would be looking for civilian jobs and housing. Another issue that would be addressed by the government would be what to do with the countries that lost the war. Betty Slentz Poole made a thought-provoking statement in her letter to Bob in her letter of January 3, 1946, when the war was over.

"President Truman is speaking now on his report of the nation. I'm anxious to hear what his ideas are on the great problems facing the United States in this post-war era. It's a decisive moment for the U.S. – as well as the whole world."

Censoring the mail ~ Dolores Herman

Letters from boyfriends were especially important to women. Many times, the censors would cut out or black out any mention of change of location. Soldiers were careful not to send any sensitive material home. Dolores Herman has a letter from her husband, Irwin, with a small paragraph that was removed from the letter.

Since there was a delay in the mail delivery, the censors let information through to family. In the case of the highly secretive atomic bomb, the bombing of Japan had already occurred when Irwin Herman wrote to Dolores. In the letter below, Irwin referred to the "scuttlebutt" of information that is going around the base where he is stationed. He is not even familiar with what the bomb can do. He is looking forward to the time to go home to family and his girlfriend, Dolores Baker.

Irwin Herman war letter

Bert Ramsey Baker~

Bertha Ramsey Baker received a sweet note from boyfriend and future husband, John.

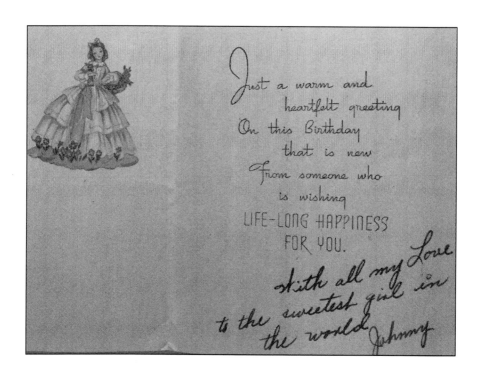

THE RED CROSS DURING WWII

"In 1881, American humanitarians Clara Barton and Adolphus Solomons founded the American Nation Red Cross, an organization designed to provide humanitarian aid to victims of wars and natural disasters in congruence with the International Red Cross." (www.history.com) According to the website History Learning, "The Red Cross played a very important role in World War Two with the help they gave to prisoners of war. They were neutral and treated anyone caught up in a conflict wherever this was." Many servicemen were greeted by the smiling faces of Red Cross volunteers in the United States and overseas.

American Red Cross

The Red Cross website states, "The Red Cross shipped over 300,000 tons of supplies overseas. Overseas, Red Cross workers were attached to military hospitals, military ships, and hospital trains. At home, millions of Red Cross volunteers provided comfort and aid to members of the Armed Forces and their families, served in hospitals suffering from severe shortages of medical staff, and produced emergency supplies for war victims." The Red Cross provided aid for prisoners of war and supplied "27 million packages for American and Allied prisoners of war."

The Red Cross had stationary and mobile service facilities during the war. "The America Red Cross Clubmobile Service was a mobile service club staffed by American women who served coffee and doughnuts to American servicemen in Europe during World War Two," stated the Harvard University Guides. Sometimes servicemen were stationed in areas where permanent clubs were not available or in a safe area for Red Cross personnel. The American History website states,

"By the end of 1945, nearly every family in America contained a member who had either served as a Red Cross volunteer, made contributions of money or blood, or was a recipient of Red Cross services." The Red Cross uniform consisted of a "cotton dress and belts with the Red Cross emblem on the front and on the matching hat." Hats and uniforms had a red cross on a white background. There were several different styles, fabrics, and colors depending on the location and the time of the year.

German Red Cross

Red Cross aid was available in other countries as well as to the United States. The German Red Cross, DRK, was founded by Dr. Aaron Silverman in Berlin, Germany. "The German Red

Cross officially came under the control of the Nazi Party in 1937." (www.histclo.com) "The Red Cross volunteers helped wounded German soldiers in the field and assisted in their treatment and recuperation. The organization through the International Red Cross assisted Germans held abroad as prisoners of war by the Western Allies and German civilians in the war damaged cities." After the war was over, Christa Stiel's family was helped by the Red Cross which located Christa's father.

Historical reenactor: Tina Lumbard

Isabella Zemer Lively

"I was born and lived in Panama for twenty-five years. In the community where I grew up, on the Pacific side of the Isthmus, there was one high school. Most of us walked to school, but some students in surrounding towns were bussed to school. World War II broke out in December 1941 of my junior year. Our school was at the foot of the hill where the Administrative offices of the Panama Canal government were located. It was a white, three-story quad building of reinforced concrete, capped with a red tiled roof, in the center of which was a courtyard in keeping with its Spanish architecture. We were greeted each morning by a freshly hoisted United States flag, reminding us of our American birthright."

"After attending Boston University, I returned to the Canal Zone and worked as Secretary to the Personnel Director of the Panama Canal Company. In 1950, I moved to San Francisco where I began my first job in the United States as Executive Secretary to George Lively at Safeway Stores, Inc."

How did WWII affect your life?

"We had rationing of food items, gasoline and tires. The Panama Canal Zone had rationing much like the United States."

What do you want America to know about your experiences?

Something that made a great impression on Isabella was the visit of President Franklin Delano Roosevelt to the Canal Zone in 1933. Even though this was prior to the beginning of WWII, events that would spark a worldwide conflict were beginning in Europe. The safety of the Panama Canal would continue to be of concern throughout the time before the war for the United States. Sabotage was a concern for the Panama Canal Zone once Germany invaded Poland on September 1, 1939.

According to the Global Security website, "Three basic measures were instituted...special equipment in the lock chambers designed to detect underwater mines and bombs." Secondly, "restriction of commercial traffic to one side of the locks." Lastly, "inspection of all ships before they entered the locks and placing of an armed guard on vessels while in transit through it."

"My seven-year old sister, Phyllis, was a polio victim, and I was nine years old. My sister remembered the exact spot she stood as President Franklin Delano Roosevelt, also a polio survivor, drove by in an open-air automobile. I was one of many who lined up holding an American flag to wave as President Franklin Delano Roosevelt came along the famous Roosevelt Avenue with its huge canopy of banyan trees. It had been named for his cousin Theodore Roosevelt, since he was our president when the United States began the construction of the Panama Canal in 1904."

"President Franklin D. Roosevelt made a total of four visits to the Panama Canal in the years 1935, 1938, and 1940 (two visits). The biggest thrill for me, however, was our mother, Mary Zemer, was commissioned to create a birthday cake to be served at the testimonial dinner at the Ancon Hospital in his honor. The Commission had selected a design requiring square-shaped pans to be made to special dimensions. Not having an oven of her own to accommodate all the cake pans, she had to bake them at the Balboa Union Church. Our house was in a complete frenzy for a few days as our 38-year old mother skillfully crafted this unique creation complete with American flags."

What did you do to help the war effort?

"I danced with the servicemen at the canteen in 1945. I wore

my Red Cross uniform and am pictured dancing with the naval boys at the canteen in Balboa, Canal Zone. The uniform had a white collar and a Red Cross emblem on the front of the dress. I volunteered at the information desk at the Red Cross also."

After the war ~

Isabella, nicknamed Miz, married George Lively in February 1956 and had a 'Lively' life for thirty-five years. When George became seriously ill, they both retired early and moved to Sonoma, California.

Author's Note ~

Sadly, Mary Isabella Zemer Lively, or Miz, passed away in Fairfield, California, on July 15, 2018 at age 92.

Phyllis Newton

How did WWII affect your life?

"Growing up, I lived in Colombia Falls, Montana, and we could get Kalispell, Montana, Calgary, Canada and Salt Lake City, Utah stations on the radio. We would try to get the Mormon Tabernacle Choir on Sundays. We had so much interference and static that we often couldn't get any radio, but the news did come over the radio on Sunday, December 7, 1941, about the attack on Pearl Harbor. I remember hearing about it in the afternoon. We were out playing in the snow talking with one of the boys who was riding his bicycle despite two feet of snow. He was the one who brought us the news. Margaret Marantette, my best friend, and I listened to what he had to say; we became very furious with Japan.

"So, I went home, and my father was there. He was only home on Saturday and Sunday because he worked in a silver mine near Eureka, Montana. He said, 'now just a minute' and he got a book off the library shelf. He brought it over to me, and it was a graph. He said, 'Phyllis, look how many people to the arable acre are in Japan' and I looked, and it was forty-six people to an arable acre. 'Now look in the United States.' It was two people to an arable acre. He said, 'This is probably why they are looking to expand.' By that time, Japan had been in Korea, China, and Malaysia. They had been a problem in the world. I learned from my dad that there are reasons that you don't think about. That's the way it was."

Another way WWII affected Phyllis' life was sugar rationing. "Sugar was a problem for us. I got extra sugar to can when I was in Bedford, Indiana,1945-1947. We had fruit trees, and my dad said, 'You have to can because that is what we live on.' You received special sugar coupons for canning, but my ration coupon book vanished. I thought, 'What in the world am I going to do?' My father said I had to can them anyway without sugar. They didn't taste good. I canned apples and cherries without any sugar. When mom and dad died, I cleaned up the library and found a book with a marker in it. The marker was my coupon book for sugar. My dad had been reading the book. So, I finally found out what happened to my coupon book. He is the one who should have known where it was, but he didn't."

"We lined up for silk stockings, and I remember getting one pair. The women were lined up around the square at Bedford to get one pair of silk hose. Nylon hadn't been invented until it was used for parachutes in the war. So, we had to have church hose, and we had to get them some way. I remember buying one pair of hose after standing in line for forty-five minutes to an hour."

What did you do for the war effort during WWII?

"I folded bandages, and I was the youngest in the group. Mrs. Ferd Green was the Red Cross leader. She had on her Red Cross outfit with a cross on the cap and the flowing, draping cloth down from the cross. She was an impressive special lady anyway. Her sons also went to war. We met every Monday night, and we would put in two hours. We would fold the bandages which were gauze. The bandages had to be kept clean. We folded them into squares. The bandages had to be folded just right, so that they got to be about four by four or three by four. We did two different kinds of bandages. Then Mrs. Ferd Green packed them very carefully. We had to be very sterile and didn't have rubber gloves. Probably, they were sterilized later. We did box after box after box. The Red Cross was doing this for the Armed Forces."

"The Red Cross also did afghans for the hospitals. I knitted squares that would be put together for the afghans, but I wasn't very good at that. I probably didn't make as many afghan squares as I should have. These things were for our people during the war. The group also knitted scarves and wool socks, but I didn't do it. I must have been a freshman in high school. This was somewhere in 1942 after the attack on Pearl Harbor. In the spring of 1942, there was a huge rubber shortage because the Japanese had taken the island of Malaysia where the rubber came from. We went scavenging around for old rubber tires."

"I babysat when I was eight years old for a quarter a night. They were the children of a scalawag electrician who told people the money was for the REM, but never put up the electric poles. I started saving my twenty-five cents to buy a war stamp. When you got eighteen dollars and seventy-five cents in your book, you traded it in for a bond. That's what I went to college on. I didn't spend money on me. We had the Sears Roebuck and Montgomery Ward catalog, but I used my money for a down payment on school and worked my way through college."

"My dad soon joined the war effort and was a very gifted craftsman. He had been a pastor, but the only sure pay he got was $350 a year for doing the religious services at the Old Soldiers Home. We had four children in the family, and I was the oldest. There just weren't many jobs in Flathead Valley where we lived. He had gone to work in the mines, but when the war hit he decided to get work at various places. He did carpentry work building barracks and things like that at a naval base in Coeur d'Alene, Idaho."

"Then he went to Hanford, Washington to work on war jobs." Hanford, Washington, was later known as the Hanford Site, a nuclear production site during WWII. In 1943, the site was created as part of the Manhattan Project to develop an atomic bomb before Germany could develop this technology.

"During this time, Dad caught pneumonia. Momma got a phone call that dad was dying and that she should come. I remember seeing her walk across the field as she went to the railroad station." Jane Rogers had agreed to stay with the children while Phyllis' mother was away. "I thought 'I have to fix something for my siblings to eat'. Momma made bread before she left." Phyllis went to the cellar to find something for dinner. She found carrots, then sliced them, put them in egg, milk and cracker crumbs. "I was frying them when Jane arrived. She said, 'Well, new cooks always try fancy stuff.' You remember these interesting details on a very difficult day."

"When Phyllis' mother arrived at the hospital, the nurses came three times to get Mama to Daddy's bedside to be there when he died. She told the doctors that he wasn't going to die because we can't get along without him. She prayed. One day the doctors said, 'We have a new drug that hasn't been tested. He is going to die anyway. So, would you give us permission to use the new sulfa drug'? That drug turned him around. This was in November, and in February he came home from the hospital."

"That Christmas was difficult. We didn't have a Christmas tree, so my good friend Margaret and I went up to the mountains to find a tree. I was a freshman in high school. We walked for miles looking for good trees. The one I brought back was really scraggly. It was the worst Christmas tree we ever had, but it was a Christmas tree. Momma and Daddy were not there because Dad was still in the hospital."

"While I was still at home, I had a special caring teacher, Mr. Bachlin. Their son, Sidney Bachlin, graduated from high school when he was sixteen. He wanted to go into the military because everybody was in the war. His parents signed for him to go into the military. He was wounded in the Battle of the Bulge and was pulled out of combat, but two weeks later he returned to combat. After that time, he was wounded again and froze to death. It was a crushing blow when this happened. We had lots of WAVES and WACs from our town. My Aunt Mary was in the WACs, but she isn't living now."

After Phyllis' dad recovered, he went to Bedford, Indiana, to work at Crane Naval Base. "My dad's parents were in their eighties and my Aunt Peggy had worked so hard and such long hours as a medical doctor that she developed nephritis and was given six months to live. Most male doctors were with the military units. My grandmother was senile, and Aunt Peggy asked my dad for help. His way of doing that was to send his oldest daughter. I went to Bedford when I was sixteen to care for my grandparents. Later my dad came, too, to work at Crane Naval Base during the war."

"My husband's brother, Jim, was at Imo Jima. He was assigned to carry the radio gear of a Navajo Code Talker who was wading ashore beside him during the landing. The fifty-pound pack he was carrying was dragging him under the water. The Navajo pulled him upright and saved Jim from drowning. At that time, a Japanese sniper shot though Jim's hand which was on his face. The shot grazed Jim's forehead which bled profusely; however, the bullet continued on to kill the man who had just saved him. Jim had bad dreams near the end of his life and probably died from PTSD, Post-Traumatic Stress Disorder."

In another instance, Phyllis told the story of another person from her small town in Montana, Peck Green, Mrs. Ferd Green's son. "Peck Green was shot down over Japan. He was taken prisoner and survived the Japanese POW camp. He married the Captain's daughter who said, 'He is not dead; he will return' and he did. He was very skinny, but alive, when he came home."

Willie and Joe Cartoons

Bill Mauldin was responsible for the creation of two GIs from WWII, Willy and Joe, Mauldin drew black and white cartoons depicted how soldiers lived but also funny situations in the war. Mauldin died in January 2003.

"The Bedford paper carried cartoons of Willy and Joe. They graphically told you what was happening at the front during the war. My favorite was a serviceman in the armored division. He had a jeep in terrible condition - the armored division was originally the cavalry - the officer was pointing his gun at the engine. You had this stuff coming out of this engine, and he was going to shoot his horse (jeep) because it had died or was in bad shape. It was so funny. He was a very good cartoonist."

When did you attend college?

"I have two degrees; I did three years in Home Economics at Purdue, but left Purdue when my husband graduated in 1950.

I returned to school at IUPUI, Indiana University Purdue University Indianapolis, when my children were adults and earned a B.S. and an M.S. in English Education with minors in Arts and Crafts. Both of my parents were graduates of Purdue University. The men in my classes at Purdue came home from the war ready to get married. I met my future husband, Gene, at Purdue. He was going to college on the GI Bill."

Berlin Crisis – 1960-62

Phyllis and Gene lived in Chambley, France, on the Chambley Air Force Base during the Berlin Crisis. "The base was located between Verdun and Metz, but it was out in the rural countryside. I was only there nine months, and I was the second woman to arrive for the whole unit. I came with three children and had to pay my way since there was a travel ban for military personnel dependents. The base was un-mothballed by the National Guard. Gene was also called up for the Korean situation." Gene did not have to go overseas during the Korean conflict because "he had a critical job as an engineer."

What was the greatest achievement in your life?

Phyllis is a very active woman in the Indianapolis, Indiana community and her church. In November 2017, she was awarded the Sagamore of the Wabash, the highest honor given to someone in Indiana, by the Governor. She has always been someone who has given back and cared for others. "The honor was having friends who thought enough of my efforts in prison ministry, and in re-entry, that they went to the trouble to find out about all the things that I had done as a Christian over the years. They put all that in the nomination asking for the award; I was the only one that didn't know anything about it. It was the most amazing thing to have friends and family like that. I taught Sunday School for more than fifty years."

"I did day camp for boy scouts and day camp for girl scouts. I was one of the originators of Timothy Churchmouse which became *Time for Timothy* on Indianapolis television." This program was a Christian television show that ran for thirty-five years from 1957-1992.

"The greatest thing you do is birth and rear a Christian family. The fact that my children and grandchildren are dedicated Christians is a wonderful thing. Every generation has to have leadership and followers. We have come a long way in my lifetime with being inclusive in church. My friend, Margaret, was a Catholic, and I was a Protestant, but Margaret couldn't come to my church. If she did, she had to go to the priest and confess that she had been in a Methodist church. We are all Christians now."

Phyllis and Gene had three natural children; however, they raised four more children. "A woman at the church was homeless and no longer able to stay in her home. She called me to come get four-year old Lester. I went and got him and months later the woman instigated neglect charges against herself so that Lester could stay here with us. We reared him until he was twenty-one. When he was about seventeen, I got a call from my sister-in-law. My brother's widow had remarried, and they had children. My brother's widow and her husband were killed in an automobile accident."

"I immediately decided to go down there and stay with the children. It was spring break, and I had to return to school ten days later. The children stayed with the Todd family for the rest of the school year; then, the children became wards of the state. They were placed with us. Donna was fifteen; John was eleven; and Charlie was nine. After spending the first day with the children, I had to sleep at Gene's aunt's home in Brownstown, Indiana, but I promised the children I would be back in the morning. Charlie said, 'I will be up when you arrive,' and I told him to just sleep because it will be six o'clock in the morning when I get there. That's too early for you. When I got there, he ran out without his coat and said. 'I told you I would be up.' The children had a difficult time facing life without their parents. They lived with us until they were grown."

Mary Jeanette Plane

What kind of things did you and your family do for the war effort?

Jeanette was in elementary and middle school during the WWII years, but she was not too young to help with the war effort. She said, "I remember knitting squares that were four by four inches that were donated to the Red Cross. Some members of the Red Cross would put the squares together to construct afghans for the soldiers." Since her mother knitted sweaters for the soldiers, Jeanette used the left-over yarn to make her squares.

"Our family bought savings bonds to help the war effort. I took my dime to school to purchase a stamp. A small stamp was ten cents and a large one was twenty-five cents. When you had enough stamps to equal $18.75, you could get a savings bond. When the bond matured, it could be redeemed for twenty-five dollars."

How did WWII affect your life?

"My brother, Jack Yates, had polio as a child and could not serve in the military. His inability to serve his country affected him for many years. Fifty years later, he apologized to the veterans at a gathering where he was the speaker. He became an ordained minister in the United Church of Christ church. I also had a cousin in the Marines who came back safely."

What do you remember about the war years?

"I remember seeing a lot of the war things on newsreels at the Washington Theater in Evansville, Indiana. They showed the ships sliding swiftly into the war on the newsreels, but my dad said the LSTs, that were built in Evansville, went into the water slowly." LSTs, Landing Ship Tanks, were built in Evansville, Indiana, from 1942 to 1945. The long ship was built to carry troops, jeeps, and supplies to the soldiers fighting in the war. Evansville, Indiana, is home to LST 325 and tours are available to the public.

Mary Jeanette Yates, Jeanette, graduated from Bosse High School in 1950; however, she was not at school to receive her diploma. After a traffic accident put her in the hospital for three weeks, two weeks in a coma, she recovered from her injuries. After awakening from the coma, she found her high school diploma on her bed. It took several months before she could use her scholarship to attend Evansville College, now University of Evansville, to continue her education. She dropped out of college after two years to marry Bob Covington. In 1967, after raising their three children, she returned to the University of Evansville to finish her degree in education. She taught elementary school for twenty-two years. After Bob's death, Jeanette married Lewis Plane, a WWII veteran who fought in the Battle of the Bulge.

What was your greatest achievement in your life?

"My college education gave me permission to teach school."

ELEANOR ROOSEVELT

"A woman is like a tea bag – you can't tell how strong she is until you put her in hot water." – Eleanor Roosevelt

Eleanor Roosevelt, wife of President Franklin Delano Roosevelt, was a compassionate advocate for WWII servicemen and their families. Mrs. Roosevelt was First Lady from March 1933 until April 1945 when President Roosevelt died. Since Eleanor Roosevelt was the First Lady of the United States during the WWII years, it would be fitting to describe her contributions to the war effort. President Roosevelt and Eleanor had four sons in the military. According to *Reminisce* magazine, "She wrote a daily syndicated newspaper column, My Day, from late 1935 until autumn 1962, shortly before her death" on November 7, 1962 in New York City, New York.

Mrs. Roosevelt visited America servicemen who had been wounded or were sick. According to the website, www.smithsonianmag.com, Mrs. Roosevelt met more than 400,000 troops during her travels in the Pacific while the Allies were fighting the Japanese army. "In October 1942, she visited Britain which was the first time a First Lady had been out of the country by herself." Her trip to Britain was considered a dangerous trip as Nazi bombers were bombing the area after she left. Not only did Mrs. Roosevelt meet with the women in the area she also visited military hospitals.

Since President Franklin Roosevelt had polio and was not very mobile, she was considered his hands and feet. Eunice Desjardins, a WWII WAVE, saw Mrs. Roosevelt once when she came to speak at WAVE Quarters D in Washington D.C. Eunice described Mrs. Roosevelt as "very influential and powerful."

According to www.history.com, "Mrs. Roosevelt advocated on behalf of European refugees who wanted to come to the United States. She also promoted issues that were important to American troops, worked to boost soldiers' morale, encouraged volunteerism on the home front, and championed women employed in defense industry." First Lady Eleanor Roosevelt was involved in helping the American people in many ways during a difficult time for the country. President and Mrs. Roosevelt, and their dog, Fala, are buried in the Rose Garden at the Franklin D. Roosevelt Library in Hyde Park, New York.

WOMEN WITH TIES TO OTHER COUNTRIES

As Americans, we tend to think in terms of our country; our American heroes, and our struggles and triumphs. Many innocent people were affected by the Axis nations' desire to rule the world. Suffering and pain spread across Europe, Asia and throughout the Pacific. One Sunday morning in December 1941 the innocence of America was changed. Hawaii was a place many people of the 1940s had never heard of or knew the exact location. It would change families forever and few people in the world would be untouched.

All the countries mentioned in this following section contain stories of strong women and children whose lives were changed by the declaration of war by the United States. Our allies, England, France, China, and Cuba, made many sacrifices to fight against Germany, Japan, and Italy. The countries of our enemy had women with victorious stories, too. It took strong women to survive this long bitter war. Among our enemy countries, there were stories of survival against a war not of their choosing. Stories of Japanese American women and children imprisoned because of their ancestry. A Romanian child who was imprisoned and abused because of her religion. British women and children who had the strength to carry on during the bombing by German planes night after night. When as a child, your normal is going to a British bomb shelter each night.

A British child, now a woman of WWII, described her mother as a "heroine" because she kept the family of ten children together. WWII created many powerful women who discovered a strength within themselves to do whatever was needed within the circumstances she found herself. In some cases, there has been a need for forgiveness to finally put some unhappy memories in the past. There are truly exceptional and talented women in all these countries.

CHINA DURING WWII

China is a large country in Asia which had continuing conflicts with Japan since 1937. When the Chinese and Japanese troops fought at the Marco Polo Bridge near Beijing, China, war started in earnest between the two countries. The United States did not become involved with Japan and China as Americans did not want to become entangled in another war. By 1940, the United States did send aid to China through the Lend Lease program.

Once the United States was attacked by Japan in December 1941, "the United States and China became allies during WWII and more than 250,000 Americans served in what was known as the "China-Burma-India" theater." The Burma Road was used to supply China with military materials by British and American governments. According to the website, www.2db.com. The route started in "Lashio, Burma (now Myanmar) to Kumming, China. Supplies arrived by ship in Rangoon (now Yangon) in Burma and traveled by rail through Mandalay to Lashio." In 1942, the road was no longer of use after being overrun by the Japanese. Supplies had to be flown over the Himalayas and became known as 'Flying the Hump.' It was a risky mission for the Allied pilots and crews. Pilots faced extreme weather conditions and high mountain peaks.

China's leader, Chiang Kai-Shek, would not surrender to Japan, even though China did not have a lot of resources nor a great army. Madame Chiang Kai-Shek was highly regarded by many and according to *Time Magazine*, "she made a rousing address to the U.S. Congress appealing for help against the Japanese. A charismatic intellectual who challenged traditional ideas of silent and subservient Chinese women" took a leading role in Chinese politics. "She was even featured three times on the cover of TIME magazine."

Madame Chiang Kai-Shek, born Soong May-ling, made an impression on American servicemen as well. One U.S. Army soldier, Herman McGregor, remarked, "I met Chiang's wife twice. She would have made a better ruler than her husband. Madame Chiang Kai-Shek gave us candy and ignored the Chinese kids that were there." However, First Lady Eleanor Roosevelt may have had a different view of Madame Chiang Kai-Shek when she said, "She can talk beautifully about democracy," Mrs. Roosevelt said later "But she does not know how to live democracy." (www.nytimes.com) It seems that Madame Chiang Kai-Shek was a complex and complicated woman.

Sophie Lee Woo

"I woke up in the morning, and it was 7:55 a.m. It was very early on December 7, 1941. On the radio it said we were being attacked. My parents and I got up because we were very nervous to hear we were being bombed. I could hear the airplanes as we had breakfast and wondered what was happening. Next door to us was this family who had been down near Pearl Harbor that morning. The girl next door told us it was pretty bad." Sophie and her family lived in Honolulu near Waikiki Beach. "I was outside with my friend next door. She put on all her jewelry. She thought that the Japanese were going to rob her of all her jewels. We were nervous all-day long. The Honolulu newspaper, The Star-Bulletin, had WAR in large letters all over the front page. We pulled the blinds at night and went to bed wondering what was going to happen the next day. The Japanese didn't come back, but we just didn't know."

"Eventually, my parents built a bomb shelter. I don't think many people did, but my parents did. It had steps going down into it. Anytime there was a siren, my mom and I would go down into it. My mother would bring oranges for us to suck on and crackers to eat. We would sit there until it was over. We went to the bomb shelter many times. Then we planted some vegetables for a victory garden. My mom planted peanuts; of course, they never developed."

Did your life change after war was declared on Japan?

Sophie was about twelve years old at the time of the bombing of Pearl Harbor. "We were always apprehensive about the war and being on the islands; we were stuck there. We weren't able to travel to the states or travel back or forth to anywhere. There wasn't any feeling of freedom anymore. I had a friend who always wore, 'I am Chinese' on her chest, so people would not mistake her for being Japanese. The best man in our wedding married a Japanese woman, and my parents were not very pleased about it. Prior to their marriage, the Japanese woman was in an internment camp in Arizona. They met at the university after the war. A lawyer took her in, and she became a housekeeper and then a teacher. Later, she met our best man and married him."

How did WWII affect your life?

"There was rationing and shortages of milk and butter. At Christmas time, mom hung Christmas bulbs on an avocado tree. We had to make do with what we had. We did mostly Chinese cooking, as my father liked to do the cooking. My mother did the driving to the university where my father worked. My father, Professor Shao Chang Lee, taught Chinese History and Culture at the University of Hawaii. The Army took over my junior high school and used it for their headquarters. We had to go to school on half sessions, so I only went to school in the afternoon leaving my mornings free. We wore gas masks to school every day. That was a big change in my life."

Leaving Hawaii ~

"Our family lived in Canton, China, before coming to Hawaii. The Chinese medical people in the states were offering three Rockefeller scholarships, and my father got one of them. My father attended Yale University, and in 1943, my father was invited to teach in Michigan. We left Hawaii and moved to East Lansing, Michigan. We had to leave on a freighter which took about eleven days to get to San Francisco. We were part of a convoy with a destroyer which circled around us for protection. There were lots of college students onboard going to the universities on the mainland."

"My mother had to buy a heavy coat for me. I had never worn a heavy coat before. I had never seen an African American person before I saw Army personnel in Hawaii. When we went to Michigan State College, we couldn't find a place to live in East Lansing. Friends found a place for my father and mother to live, but there was not enough room for me. I stayed in San Francisco for a year and attended high school. After that time, I was able to move to East Lansing, Michigan, with my family."

"In Hawaii, everyone was supposed to work. I worked at a gift shop and some at the pineapple factory. When we came to the United States during the summer, I got a job at Winona Lake in Indiana. I lived in a dormitory with three girls from Scandinavia. We all worked in the camp cafeteria for a small wage, but it wasn't hard work. The people who attended the camp were from the Chicago area. We had afternoons to go swimming in the lake. The war ended in 1945, and my friend called and said, 'The war is over.' I returned home to Michigan. My father taught at Michigan State College, later Michigan State University, in East Lansing. I went two years to Michigan State College and finished at University of Michigan with a B.S. in Nursing."

What do you want America to know about your experiences?

"When my family moved to Michigan, people were very friendly. Also, when I enrolled in high school, they were very nice and friendly. One of the girls thought I would be in pigtails. This is what she had seen in pictures. They invited me over for dinner and sleepovers, but I was different because I was Chinese. Hawaii had been very multi-cultural."

"In 1949, I met my husband, Robert Kwoh Tao Woo, who was from Beijing, China. He received two degrees in Mechanical Engineering from the University of Michigan and worked at Ford Motor Company. He had a green card because he was not a citizen yet."

What was your greatest achievement?

"I was fortunate to marry someone from China and to have the wonderful kids that I have. I had a daughter first, then a son. They have been able to attend universities without any difficulties. I had such a happy marriage and life. Life has been good."

Sophie did not return to Hawaii until she was seventy years old. She found it to be very different from what she remembered. One of the men whom she knew as a young boy still lived next door on her old street in Honolulu.

Author's Note~

Sadly, Sophie passed away quietly on August 31, 2018. According to her obituary of Sunday, September 2, 2018, "The first decade of her life was spent with the Donaldina Cameron House, a mission community for Chinese girls. In 1938, she was taken in by Prof. Shao Chang Lee and his wife, Nora Wong Lee."

CUBA DURING WWII

The island of Cuba which is called the "Pearl of the Antilles" lies southeast of the United States. It is about one hundred miles from Key West, Florida, the southernmost point of the United States. Cuba has been an ally of the United State and during WWII the United States maintained a naval base at Guantanamo Bay. According to the website Enotes.com, "Cuba was officially a member of the allied nations during WWII, declaring war on, first Japan, and then Germany and Italy shortly after the bombing of Pearl Harbor."

Relations with Cuba have not always been friendly. During WWII, Cuba was used for postal operations and a distribution area for merchant shipping convoys. Many Cubans would prefer the United States return the control of Guantanamo Bay Naval Base to the Cuba government, much like President Carter did with the Panama Canal while he was in office. In December 1999, the Panama Canal was given to Panama after the United States controlled its operation since 1914.

German Spies in Cuba

According to the website, www.urrib2000.narod.ru, during 1943 a Cuban anti-submarine ship SC-13, with the aid of the American Kingfisher, sank the German sub U-176 when it was discovered that a "German spy that worked in Havana [was] transmitting information to his submarines. The spy was executed." During war time, it was common for informants to infiltrate into an enemy country to gather critical information for their own country. Heinz Luning, a German citizen who became a spy for the Nazis during WWII, was well known; however, he did not reveal any real secrets to the Nazis about the Allies in Cuba. He was sent to Cuba to spy but was not very good about sending messages to Germany, so he was discovered and executed for spying.

Cuba today~

Beginning in July 2015, the United States restored diplomatic relations between Cuba and the United States. Thus, easing the difficult and hostile relationship between the two countries since 1961. Fidel Castro ruled the country for many years, and the current Cuban president is Raul Castro. Havana, the largest and the capital city, houses the United States embassy. Since 2002, Guantanamo has contained a military prison for enemies of the United States who were captured during the Afghanistan and Iraq wars.

Mercedes Cros Sandoval

In November 1933, Mercedes Cros was born in Cuba to a family whose father was a highly educated man with an interest in Archeology. "My father read a lot and was a very smart man."

"When I was a child, we had the radio on listening to Radio Warsaw. They were playing Chopin's 'Revolutionary Polonaise'. It was played over and over, when suddenly, the radio went silent. We could hear gunfire, and then the German military march was playing on the radio. We knew WWII had started – September 1, 1939." Hitler invaded Poland and took control of the country. Later, all Jews, Gypsies, and a lot of Polish people were rounded up and sent to concentration camps. "When I was about five or six years old, my mother told me to pray every night that the war would be over. I prayed every night."

"In approximately 1938-39, my father, Dr. Juan Cros, who was a physician and a snail expert, was contacted by a German man from the University of Hamburg in Hamburg, Germany. The German man came to see my father and asked for assistance with his research on Cuban orchids. The German stayed around two years in Cuba and travelled out in the countryside with my father sometimes. My father, being a doctor, often travelled to the countryside to see his patients."

"On one occasion, my father, mother, and I were travelling by boat from Baraco to Santiago. The German man boarded the boat and told us that he had received a phone call from Germany. His mother was sick, and he was leaving Cuba. My father told my mother, 'Something is wrong.' My father said, 'I am afraid that a war is about to start.' There were no phone connections from Cuba to Germany in those days."

"This German man was doing more than orchid research." Mercedes said when remembering the German man, "Later, we found out the German man was probably measuring the depths of the little bays around Baracoa. This idea was later proved to be possible because German subs were used to get into this area to attack American Navy boats stationed at Guantanamo Bay. My parents and I suspected the German man was a spy."

How did WWII affect your life?

Like the United States and England, Cuba experienced rationing of many daily items. "I remember we didn't have toothpaste and butter. We made butter at home."

What do you want America to know about your experiences?

"Cubans were a very happy people, but the war impacted everyone. At the movies, I saw the war newsreels. I was horrified to see the concentration camps. There were pictures of bodies in magazines, too. Cuba declared war on Germany and Japan. The United States and Cuba were allies. Some Cuban-American men who lived in America volunteered to go to war. It was not possible for Cuban men to join the United States military unless they lived in the United States. There was a song that we sang when Japan was destroyed."

Pin Pin Cayo Berlin
Pin Pin Cayo Japon
Hirohito is crying because
MacArthur rode his white horse

Do you remember when WWII ended?

"I was in Santiago, Cuba, and there were many people in the streets. It sounded like a roar of voices."

In 1951-52, Ms. Sandoval studied Social Sciences at the University of Havana. "I dated a man who was in the United States Navy. I liked him a lot; however, when I left to study in Havana, he fell in love with someone else."

Life in the United States ~

"In 1955, I moved to Tallahassee Florida to study Anthropology. I have not been back to Cuba. I love Cuba, but I love the United States more and have gratitude for all the opportunities I have. Castro destroyed Cuba. Communism doesn't work because they don't know how to do things. The more people are paid, the more they work. There was a struggle between Fascism and Communism. When I moved to the United States, I didn't realize the choices I could make. Envy destroyed my nation – Cuba."

What was your greatest achievement in your life?

"I am a hell of a good teacher. I love my students...all my life." Ms. Cros Sandoval taught classes on feminism at Grinnell University. She has written four books and contributed many research articles to scientific magazines. Two books she has written are *Worldview, the Orichas, and Santeria: Africa to Cuba and Beyond, and Mariel and Cuban*

National Identity. She learned several foreign languages and lived in Madrid, Spain, for four years. Anthropologist Mercedes Cros Sandoval's background includes professor emeritus at Miami Dade College and adjunct professor in the Department of Psychiatry at the University of Miami.

What do you have to say about WWII women?

"WWII was an awakening for women."

ENGLAND DURING WWII

England was a member of the Allies along with France during WWII and joined later by the United States. Once Hitler invaded Poland and other European countries, England and France declared war on Germany September 3, 1939. Winston Churchill, Prime Minister of England, met with American President Franklin Roosevelt during the early years before the United States entered the war. England was heavily burdened to fight a war with Germany. President Roosevelt wanted to help Britain, without becoming involved in the war, so in March 1941 he signed the Lend Lease Bill. Essentially, this meant according to *www.history-state.gov*, "The United States would provide Great Britain with the supplies it needed to fight Germany but would not insist upon being paid immediately." Great Britain needed the aid and supplies but did not have the cash available to pay for military armaments.

Battle of Britain

The Battle of Britain began July 10, 1940 and ended October 31, 1940. Britain had to endure bombing by the Germans for many months. In 1940, Germany used night time bombing, or blitz, to terrorize the residents of London. According to the Britannica website, the blitz began in September 1940 and continued until May 1941. These night time bombing attacks were commonly referred to as the *Blitz*. *Blitzkreig* is the German word for 'lightning,' which forced many families to send their children to the countryside for their protection. Many Londoners took cover in the Underground or subway tunnels to avoid the attacks from the Germans.

Barrage Balloons

Barrage Balloons were used by the British to help protect London and other major city in England from enemy dive bombers. The balloons were very large and made it more difficult for the bombers to identify targets that were to be destroyed. According to the website, www.worldwar-two.net, "The barrage balloon was simply a bag of lighter-than-air gas attached to a steel cable anchored to the ground. The balloon could be raised or lowered to the desired altitude by a winch. Its purpose was ingenuous: to deny low-level airspace to enemy aircraft." Also, the steel cable holding down the balloon was a danger to planes which also deterred low level attacks. "If a balloon was shot it exploded, taking the aircraft with it." (www.bbc.co.uk)

Wendy Dutnall Howell

In 1931, Wendy was born in the county of Kent, England, which is forty miles southeast of London, England. "I was reared in an environment of news and politics. My mother, Sheila, was a teacher of five to seven-year olds which was called infants in England. She had fifty-four students in her class without a teaching assistant. When WWII started in England in 1939, Wendy was a Protestant eight-year old school "day girl" attending a Catholic Convent school. She rode her bike to school and back home in the afternoon. "Later in 1940, when the Germans were bombing this area, an aircraft would suddenly appear when I was riding home, and I would be scared. It was harassment really."

Barrage Balloons

"Barrage balloons were permanently stationed in many large cities in England to stop the dive bombers from attacks. In 1940, it was a very hot summer. I remember looking into the sunset toward London, some forty miles away, and seeing hundreds of barrage balloons."

Spitfires

Spitfires airplanes were used against the German formation of bombers. "The pilots of the Spitfires saved our lives during the Battle of Britain in 1940. Many of our seventeen and eighteen-year old men were pilots. One German bomber crashed near my town on the road. My father said, 'We must have a look.' So, we piled into the car and went to look at the perfect crash landing. Many people had taken souvenirs from the German plane."

What is a funny event that you recall?

"One of the Irish teachers at our school, Miss O'Carroll, who could be described as all jovial and talkative with protruding teeth. She wore a black felt hat with a brim, fashionable at the time, and a belted coat. She told the class about her recent visit to Southern Ireland. When she returned to Northern Ireland, she secretly carried a large package of pork sausages under her hat."

How did WWII affect your life?

"I was sent to my grandmother's house for about six months during the initial bombing and panic. My grandmother lived about thirty-five miles from our home. When I returned to my home, I witnessed the massive formation of heavy German bombers who followed the Thames River to attack London which was forty miles away. It was safer and provided some relief from the war time anxiety. On cloudy days, a single German bomber would appear out of the low clouds and attack anything it could see. This was a new technique used by the Germans."

"Rationing started from the beginning of the war and continued to well after the war. I remember that we could have five ounces of sweets. There was no chocolate. When I am sick now, I crave a banana because there were no bananas during the war. Coffee was partly British nuts – *ersatz*, a German word that meant it wasn't real coffee."

"CAMP Coffee was a good brand that contained a syrup that was mixed with hot water to make coffee. The label had a picture of a Scotsman wearing a kilt on it." There were many other things that were rationed or difficult to find. "There was no sugar or butter, unless you knew someone on a farm. There was a limit on meat." To obtain food, "there were long queues of people. Also, clothing was limited and had to last a long time."

What did your family do during bombing raids?

"Air raid shelters were used during large air invasion of enemy bombers when they were spotted. The German bombers had very noisy engines, and the sky would be dark with them. Our family had an Anderson Shelter. The one we had was galvanized metal. You had to dig a big hole and put soil on top of it. You went down into it. We put in a seat or some bunks, where I slept during the night bombings. When we heard the air raid siren, we would go to the shelter. My dad, who had very good hearing of high-pitched sounds, would say, 'take cover, they are coming.' We would dash under the oak dining room table, if we were in the house and didn't have time to get to the shelter."

"In London there were night time bombings called the Blitz. The people were very tired after night after night of going to the shelters and the underground stations, or Tubes. On cloudy nights, the Germans didn't bomb the city, and it was a great relief to the people of London. There were search lights lighting up the sky searching for German bombers. If they caught enemy planes, the guns at Chitney Marshes would go off."

What did your family do for the war effort?

"My father, George, was a Civil Defense Officer on the Isle of Sheppey. The word Sheppey means sheep. There were four anti-aircraft placement guns at Chitney Marshes to protect the coastline. The sound of the gun when fired carried to my house and sounded like the heavens were bursting. One day my father was driving near there, when he had to stop his car and take cover. Otherwise the dive bomber would have gotten him. We collected shrapnel the next day from the fragments of the shells that were shot at the German bombers."

"My grandmother knitted Balaclava helmet covers for the troops. They are knitted around the face to keep the neck warm. My grandmother helped me to knit a helmet cover, but she had to straighten it out before it could be sent to the soldiers." Wendy laughed. "My sister, Ninette, volunteered for the Women's Royal Air Force (WRAF) when she turned seventeen. My father was not very pleased about it. Ninette was eight years older than me. She was sent to the farthest most part of Scotland where it was very cold and bleak. The nearest town was Thurso. She worked on the beginning of RADAR, or as it was called then, Radio Location. She wouldn't really say what she did even to the family because it was top secret. Later Ninette married a WWII Marine from the United States and moved to America."

Buzz Bombs~

Buzz bombs were unmanned bombs that were directed at England by the German army. "One night while I was in bed, suddenly there was this terrible bright white light. Following that, was this giant rattle in the night. We knew that when the engines cut off, they would glide on until they dropped. We were staying at my grandparents' house for a brief visit.

We (my family) gathered in my grandfather's big study which had sandbags on the outside to protect the house. I remember sitting there for a while. The buzz bombs were a quite new weapon and very scary. It was a frightening noise. Another time, when I was about ten years old, I sat in my garden and saw a buzz bomb gliding by. When one was coming, there was a terrible racket. The engine cut out, but it went on. I heard it explode some distance away. You never knew where it was going to drop."

Rockets ~

"The final method of attack were the V-2 rockets sent to attack England. The Germans built rocket placements all the way up the coast to France where they sent rockets to attack us. One of the first reports was there was some mysterious new weapon that had exploded near the Isle of Sheppey. My father talked about the mysterious explosion, and he was responsible for having it cordoned off. Defense experts collected the pieces to see how it was designed."

What was your greatest achievement in your life?

"To have survived this long, and to be in the position to recognize and be vividly aware of major events after the war, up to now."

Lilian "Midge" Thilthorpe

The war in Europe and England started several years before it came to America. In 1933, Adolf Hitler came to power in Germany and began his plan to take over the world. Hitler invaded Poland on September 1, 1939; England declared war on Germany a few days later.

How did WWII affect your life?

"I was just a kid when we lived in a small country village, Kings Langley, in Hertfordshire, England, which is outside of London. My parents, Frederick and Rose Crowhurst, moved our family from London four years before the war started. When the war started, it was kind of exciting because our little village was full of military personnel and vehicles. The local football ground was an encampment. Tents everywhere!! Of course, it meant we lost our play area; still we used other spaces and the soldiers tolerated us. There were many drawbacks like being restricted in our movements, as mothers were always anxious for our well-being with all the equipment around and much more traffic on the roads. This lasted for quite a while; then suddenly they were all gone, and it was back to a quiet, boring village again."

"We had lots of children from London who had been evacuated from the city and came to live in our village. There was competition between the Londoners and the locals. Each one would say something like, 'We are better than you.' Some of the London children were in the village for two or three years before their mothers came to get them."

"Life became extremely hard for us when rationing was brought in, especially for our mother with ten children to bring up. I used to love eating sandwiches made with golden syrup or with condensed milk called conarny. My father had a large garden of vegetables and fruit trees. Mom would swap butter for lard or margarine because she could use it better. Families kept chickens and rabbits to supplement the meat and egg shortage. Even these things were restricted by the government because only a certain number of chickens and eggs were permitted. We never went hungry and always had clothes on our backs and shoes on our feet."

"Actually, we were much fitter in those days, I think, and healthier. We played outside: no television or electronic games. We just had ordinary outdoor entertainment, such as, football, cricket, tennis, hockey, chase, hide-and-seek, to name a few. With having to make our own entertainment, I am sure we were far happier than the children of today."

"I was between nine and twelve years old during this time, and we were scared at first, then excited by the raids. Night times were not good with the air raids and having to go to shelters. We would move to the air raid shelters at John Dickinson Paperworks, where my father worked, at dark and wait until the sirens stopped. We were listening to the German bombers passing overhead and hoping they did not release their bombs over us. We could hear the planes bombing London. We knew by the drone of the engine whether they were British, American or German planes. We did have a couple bombs fall quite close which was scary. The next day gave us fun looking over the rubble for shrapnel pieces when the wardens and police were not nearby. Guess we were not perfectly behaved."

"I remember one day when a group of us went up to Bluebell Woods, and as we walked back home, we watched lots of planes: Spitfire, Hurricanes, and German Fighters whirling and swirling around in the sky. It was really great for us to see, but not for our mothers anxiously waiting outside the houses urging us to quickly get inside. Naturally, we thought it more interesting to watch the air battle! I suppose, we were saddened in a way when peace came, and life went back to being boring again, although the hardships went on for quite some years. We did not appreciate it then, but our mothers were truly heroines."

Family in the war~

"One day my mom's youngest brother came home from the military. He just walked in the door looking dirty and scruffy. My mom and her sister went crazy. They asked, 'When do you have to go back?' He said, 'I don't know if I have to go back; the military thinks I am dead.' He had been at the fighting in Dunkirk, and he did go back."

What do you remember about the Americans in England?

"As a child, it was exciting watching large American planes, the Flying Fortresses, flying over and the airmen bailing out from their planes. When some of the planes were too badly damaged to return to the airport, the pilots would parachute near our house. Sometimes they might incur a broken leg or other minor injury, but usually they landed successfully. One time in the summer, an American airman parachuted out of his plane, slid down a hayrick, or haystack, onto a family's picnic table. Also, we loved the American soldiers as they were our buddies. They were very good to the kids and gave us chocolate bars and chewing gum."

Do you remember when the war ended?

"I was in my middle teens and remember there were bells ringing and a street party. There were tables down the center of the street. There was food to eat which was made or bought by all the people on the street. The kids were given special treats, and we wore red, white, and blue hats. There were flags and music blaring with dancing. Also, four men from our village came home from Japanese prisoner of war camps, and they were just skin and bones."

What is your greatest achievement in your life?

"My greatest achievement would be my three children. We had a daughter and then twin boys."

Midge and Karen

In 1950, Midge joined the WRAF, Women's Royal Air Force, and was in the service for seven years. During this time, she met her future husband, Geoff, who served over thirty years in the RAF, Royal Air Force. In 1956-57, Geoff and Lilian (Midge) met and were later married. Midge lives in England but her daughter, Karen, married an American, so Midge comes to the United States regularly for a visit.

British and American Women Aviators ~

Famous British Aviator - Lettice Curtis

During a time when women were not considered able to fly planes, Lettice Curtis was proving men wrong. She was one of one hundred-sixty-six female ATA, Air Transport Auxiliary, who ferried Royal Air Force planes. "ATA pilots were expected to deliver aircraft to wherever they were needed..." according to *The Independent* website. As a well-respected pilot, "She joined the ATA in the summer of 1940 and graduated to flying all types of wartime aircraft and was one of the first to fly heavy bombers."

She was the first woman trained on four-engine bombers. Lettice flew Lancasters, Spitfires, and Liberators. She had a special interest in aviation nearly all her adult life. She was a leader and an amazing example to other women. As a well-respected aviator, "She joined the ATA in the summer of 1940 and graduated to flying all types of wartime aircraft and was one of the first to fly heavy bombers."

British Aircraft

Spitfire - The Spitfire began flying in August 1938. By 1940, it was in full service with the RAF, Royal Air Force. The wings contained Browning machine guns and the plane was used primarily as a high and low altitude fighter. "The Spitfire was the iconic aircraft of the Battle of Britain and became the symbol of British defiance in the air." www.iwm.org.uk

Lancaster – The Lancaster was a four-engined heavy bomber used for reconnaissance. The Lancaster began flying in January 1941. A description of this plane would be, "the Lancaster was outfitted with no fewer than 8 x 7.7 mm Browning machine guns for self-defense."

Liberators – The B-24 Liberator is an American four-engined strategic heavy bomber. It was the most produced American plane used during WWII. The Liberator was favored by many pilots. The British called the plane "Liberator" so it was accepted as part of the name from that time. There was usually a crew of seven to ten men aboard.

The WASP Program – Jacqueline Cochran, American Pilot

Jacqueline Cochran was an accomplished pilot during WWII. According to the Biography website, "In June 1941, Cochran became the first woman to fly a bomber across the North Atlantic. General Arnold asked her to travel to England and observe the "Wings for Britain" program, an organization that flew American-built aircraft to Britain. In July 1943, Cochran was appointed to the General Staff of the U.S. Army Air Forces to direct the Women Airforce Service Pilots (WASP) program and trained women pilots for the duration of the war."

"Jacqueline Cochran took thirteen women pilots over to England. She went to England to see what the women were doing in England with the Royal Air Force. Some of them stayed over there and flew for the RAF Auxiliary. They were the only ones out of the country. The Ferry Command WASP took some planes up to the Canadian Border where male pilots flew them to Alaska for the Russian women to fly the planes to Russia."

FRANCE DURING WWII

France, located in western Europe, had the misfortune of being in the way of Hitler's expansion program. In 1939, Germany invaded Poland and France and Great Britain declared war against Germany. According to France-Pub.com, "The Battle of France is used to describe the invasions of the Netherlands Belgium, Luxembourg and then France by the German army." In the following months, British troops retreated, and France fell to Germany. By June 14, 1940, Paris was occupied by Axis forces and France surrendered to Germany. By October 1940, all Jews were banished from France and forced into internment camps.

German occupied France~

"During 1942, the Obligatory Work Service began throughout German occupied Europe, young men were called to participate in the war effort. The German powers demanded France provide two hundred fifty thousand volunteers." French workers were needed to fuel Germany's need for men and resources to fight the war. The German government set up a biased government sympathetic to the Germans called Vichy France.

French Resistance ~

"During the summer of 1943, there was a surge to join the French resistance and avoid the forced labor. More than thirty thousand escaped France into Spain or North Africa. Some of the young French men and women hid in homes or at farms with the help of local people. "Certain people were simply forgotten as the German bureaucracy was submerged in paper work."

The French Resistance or French Underground was a group of men and women who secretly resisted the German dominance in France. They gave information to the Allies as well as destroying and disrupting German communication and supplies. According to the website, History Learning Site, "Between January and June 1943, there were 130 acts of sabotage against rail lines each month. By September 1943, this had increased to 530." The resistance supplied the Allies with intelligence about the movements of the German army. Charles De Gaulle called upon occupied French people to unite and fight the Germans in the French Resistance. After four years of Nazi occupation, France was liberated on August 24, 1944.

Helen Lagarde

Helen's mother, Marguerite, a French citizen, married Leroy Null, a WWI soldier. After they were married, they boarded a ship to the United States. After WWI Marguerite was one of the first women to leave France and go with her husband. She became an American citizen, and Marguerite and Leroy lived in Youngstown, Ohio, where Helen was born. While visiting family in France, Marguerite received divorce papers from Leroy. She did not return to America, instead she and her seven-year old daughter, Helen, stayed in France. "I attended school in France and learned to speak French." Helen had to quit school in France to help support her mother. Helen, a teenager during WWII, became a victim of circumstances.

What was it like for you in France?

When Helen was older, she worked in a men's clothing shop in Bayonne, France. "Bayonne is an enchanting place located at the south west corner of France near the Atlantic Ocean. The climate is ideal, and the view of the mountains and the sea is beyond compare. It is at the very edge of le Pay Basque."

One day Helen met her fiancé, Jean, pronounced John, when she was working in a shop. "He came in with his older sister. I looked at him and thought he looks pretty nice. Blonds were very unusual in this area. Later that day, I was supposed to meet my friends to celebrate Bastille Day, but Jean was there where I was to meet my friends. So that was it!"

"Jean was born in French West Africa and was in the French underground." Helen didn't know what exactly he did during the war. She did know that he had his healthy appendix removed, so that he wouldn't be sent to work for the Germans. His good friend, a surgeon, performed the operation. During this time the Germans were taking healthy French men to work for them. So, Jean left France and joined his brother in North Africa for a time. Jean's brother was a high-ranking soldier in the French military. It was a way to get some military training from his brother." After Jean left France, he got word to Helen about what had happened to him. There are few details, as he didn't talk about it very much.

"The sad times came, and we were at war with Germany. In 1939, the French could not hold the Germans back, and France was invaded from Paris all the way south down the coast to where we were in Bayonne."

The Germans arrive in Bayonne, France

The Germans occupied France by mid-1940 and France signed a formal surrender June 24, 1940. Helen recalled how the Germans entered Bayonne. "That's the worst thing that can hit you when you are standing outside. We were standing on the sidewalk, and we saw their cars coming in. The German soldiers were standing on the outside of the cars with a German flag draped on the front of the car. They were looking at you like, 'see, here we are.' It gave me a feeling in my stomach. It was chilling to see, and people watched in fear and tears."

"Jewish people had to wear a star on their arms in our town. I had Jewish friends who were good to me in the town. I worked for the Jewish people who owned the clothing store where I worked." Many changes came to Bayonne with the presence of the German soldiers. "Girls who associated with the German soldiers had their heads shaved."

Arrested by the Germans

"There were so many French working for the Germans, that you couldn't trust anyone. People knew that I had been born

in the United States, and someone said something to the Germans. One morning my mother went to the country to buy lard and things." There were two German soldiers asking about Helen. "When I came home, my step-dad, Jacques Grobli, who was Swiss and spoke German, said, 'They are coming for you. You are going to have to go with them. You are going north of France.' The soldiers were human because they said to my step-dad, 'maybe something could be done.' So, they felt sorry for me. The soldiers took me to a school, and they were all sitting there in an office."

They started talking to her in French and German, but she didn't answer. "Some of the soldiers went to get some coffee for me. They were treating me kindly, and a big wheel (German officer) tried to talk to me. I was to go with a chauffeur in a black car. They were going to send me north to Germany – who knows where. The German fellow who gave me some coffee felt sorry for me. I saw the German Officer, who looked terrible, get in the car, and a woman got in the back seat. She started talking to me in English. I acted like I didn't understand. As it turned out, that was a good thing, as I suspect she was an American spy for the Germans."

"We went to the train station, and it was loaded with Americans. I assume they were being sent to prisoner of war camps. A lot of wealthy Americans lived in that part of France (Bayonne). They were looking at me and wondering why they were keeping me on the side. I couldn't figure that out either. The Americans were whispering to each other. The mean-looking German sat next to the chauffeur. We met with other Germans. The other side of the room was loaded with Americans that had been picked up before I was. The Americans that were sitting with me talked to me, but I didn't

answer them either. There could have been spies sitting with them."

"After that they said I could go home, but I had to come back every two days and sign in. I couldn't leave the town, so I grabbed my bag and left the train station. When I got outside, my step-father and Jean were waiting for me. I signed in for two days, and then the Germans said, 'You don't have to come back anymore.'"

Jean Lagarde

The Germans leave Bayonne, France

"After the Germans left Bayonne, we saw American planes coming over. My fiancé, Jean, and I were going to work when we heard a humming sound that I will never forget. It was the Americans. You could see the American flag on the wings. I told my husband-to-be that I had to go back to tell my mother that the Americans are here. She was at the window when I got back home. The sight was beautiful, hundreds of them like silver birds flying over the city. I guess you never forget it. I was about eighteen years old at the time."

Americans arrive in Bayonne, France

"When the Americans arrived, you could see the whales in the river. That same night, Jean and I took a walk to the river. We found ships there: one was English and one American. I got to talk to the captain of the American ship. He invited us aboard the ship for dinner in the Captain's Quarters. The crew was not permitted to leave the ship. The captain asked if I could buy gifts for them; they all wanted perfume. I did the shopping and the men were all thrilled. The captain gave me a can of vegetables." According to www.baleinesendirect.org, "Some species of toothed whales frequent freshwater environments (rivers, lakes)."

After the war was over, "a former German soldier and his mother came into the shop where I was working. He wanted me to meet his mother and perhaps marry him. I told him I had a boyfriend and was not interested."

How did WWII affect your life?

"Some of the things you never forget are the sounds of the

German boots. The German soldiers would walk the streets every night, always three of them together. If they would see a light, they would shout in German to put everything out. We had drapes over our windows. They would hammer at the door of our apartment building. You can't forget it. The English planes would fly by in the night, and the Germans didn't want them to see lights."

"There was a lot of sadness. Sometimes there are things you don't get anymore, some things that are gone forever, people you don't get to see any more." After the war Helen's mother and stepfather moved to Switzerland. Helen didn't see them for over twenty years until Helen returned to France for a visit. During this visit, Helen discovered that someone who had lived in her apartment building had been helping Jews escape the German occupied France.

Coming to America~

"Happier times were to come. Jean and I were engaged that Christmas." Jean and Helen were married by the mayor of the town. In 1945, they decided to leave France with their first child, John. "We had to take a train to get to the ship and come to America. I saw the Statue of Liberty from the ship. That impresses you…it is quite a feeling. I had an aunt, uncle and grandparents who lived in America. My grandfather was the sweetest man, but my grandmother was something else; she was a witch. He had to hide his food from his wife (Helen's paternal grandmother)."

In 1947, their daughter Maureen was born in Indianapolis, Indiana. "As soon as the five-year time requirement was met, Jean, and our son John became United States citizens. He was so proud." Jean and Helen were blessed with fifty-four years of marriage before Jean's death in 1997.

What was your greatest achievement in your life?

"My greatest achievement was having my children."

GERMANY DURING WWII

Adolf Hitler became Chancellor of Germany in 1933, and by 1939 he was directing troops to take over Poland, the Netherlands, Belgium, and Luxembourg; France was next to become part of Hitler's plan for world domination. Germany was part of the Axis powers along with Italy and Japan. After occupying these captured countries, the Nazis forced the citizens to work in labor camps or join the German army. In the case of the Jews, Hitler ordered them to concentration camp or labor camps. Hitler was responsible for the death of millions of Jewish people throughout Europe.

Major battles~

The war began to turn in favor of the Allies following the D-Day Invasion at Normandy, France, in June 1944. There was heavy fighting and many deaths on the beaches following the invasion. Later in the war, the Battle of the Bulge which included severe hardship for troops dealing with the cold weather took place from December 1944 to January 1945. The Battle of Berlin was the final offensive in Europe which ended May 2, 1945.

Prisoners of war~

German prisoners of war were interrogated and many of them were sent to the United States to work in camps. Following the terms of the Geneva Convention, German prisoners were treated well and allowed certain privileges; however, this was not always the case for American prisoners in Germany and Japan.

The surrender of Germany~

V-E Day, Victory in Europe, considered a major milestone in ending WWII, took place on May 8,1945. Many Americans celebrated with parades and parties hoping their loved ones would come home soon. The United states and its allies would direct all military resources to defeating Japan in the Pacific.

Death of Hitler~

Officially, Adolf Hitler's death is listed as April 30, 1945, and cause of death as suicide in Berlin, Germany. There has been speculation that he escaped and lived in South America. No definitive proof has ever been uncovered.

Christa "Christine" Stiel

How did WWII affect your life?

"As a child living in Gleiwitz, Germany, we could see the smoke coming from the concentration camp of Auschwitz nearby. My father, Stefan, used to remark to the family 'smoke is up again,' referring to the crematoriums at Auschwitz which was not far from our home. I remember seeing the Jewish children wearing a yellow star on their clothing. In Germany, a child had to pass a test to continue to middle school from elementary school. I passed one hundred per cent and attended the middle school until Christmas." Christine, or Christa, was not able to finish school in her village because of the threat of the Russians taking the village.

"On January 21, 1945, I was fifteen years old and left our village on the train as the Russians were advancing toward us. The Nazis were still there, but the Russians were a bigger concern. I remember my father saying to us, 'Get ready to leave; this is the last train before the Russians arrive in the village.'" So, Christine, her sisters, Edith and Ermgard, her brother, Alfred, and her mother, Gertrud, boarded the train to leave Gleiwitz. Christine's father and grandfather stayed behind.

"Our first night, we stopped in Sohnberg, Germany, where we stood in line for a small bowl of soup. We were only able to take a small bag with us on the train. We stayed a couple days and slept on the floor of the gymnasium with other families. Since we didn't have any money, people were kind enough to give us a small amount of food. We couldn't leave the gymnasium to go outside and play."

"When I was sixteen years, I had to register with the Czechs. I tried to leave, after registering with the Czechs, to tell my mother where I was going and couldn't come back to the gymnasium. As I was leaving to tell my mother where I was going, an official stopped me and said that something bad would happen if I left. The Czechs transported my older sister, Edith, and me to a farm owned by a Jewish man whose wife and two children had been sent to a concentration camp. He was a very nice man and very kind to us."

"I had to work out in the fields, picking corn, potatoes, weeding, and cleaning up. I had to be up working by six o'clock in the morning; we worked until one or two in the afternoon. There were cattle and crops on the farm. We were able to correspond by mail to let my mother know where we were."

"My sister was sick and weak and was given permission to work inside the house. My mother arrived and asked the farmer if she could take my sister and me with her. We went back to the gymnasium to live for a while. We had to leave the village and go to a safer place. We boarded a train which was very full, and we were told the passengers were Germans on vacation. The Germans were wearing yellow ribbons. We had seats on the train and were fed but were not given much food. The train stopped all day and all night before we crossed the border. If it hadn't stopped, we would have ended up in Russia."

"We had to get off the train when it stopped. My mother, my brother, my sisters, and I were walking through the woods, being led by two men who were going to get us to the border. It was winter time and very cold. I was very cold and wet, but we were led to a home where a very nice lady let us stay for a few hours to get warm. She gave us something hot to drink. We were told we needed to cross the border very early in the morning, around five o'clock, due to the lights and being seen." The area where Christine and her family fled was being taken over by Russian troops. The area where they were going was not infiltrated by the Russians.

"After crossing the border, we went to several different villages trying to find a good place to live. In Rangasburg, one of the villages, I washed dishes in a restaurant. My family finally settled in Kronach, Germany, living in a Festung with other families. We had our own one-bedroom apartment with a kitchen on the fourth floor, but we had to share a bath with other families. Throughout our journey, we were forced to ask people for food, and I knitted as a way to make some money."

According to Revolvy website, "German World War II strongholds were selective towns and cities." The German word festung means fortress. Merriam-Webster states, a festung was "used for defense in the part of Europe occupied by Nazi Germany against British and American invasion."

What happened to your father?

"My father and grandfather stayed behind when we left Gleiwitz. We did not know where the men of the village were while we were travelling around Germany. We found out later that the Russians took the village men to Russia to work for them. My father and another man were the only men to return from Russia. We were told by people in the village to talk to the Red Cross, and maybe they could help us find our father. After about two years, with the help of the Red Cross, our family was reunited."

Christine Meets Adam~

"As a young woman after the war, I made parts for televisions by hand, not machine. One of the families that lived in our Festung had a visitor from Canada. Adam Stiel was on vacation in Kronach visiting his uncle. Adam Stiel also had a difficult life as a young man. Adam was born in Yugoslavia, now Croatia, and grew up in Austria. His father was killed by the Nazis, and Adam had to join the German army during the war. Adam was captured in Italy and spent some time in an English POW camp for four or five months."

Christine and Adam dated for four or five weeks and were engaged. They moved to Canada and were married in a Catholic Church on November 19, 1960. Many of Adam's friends were present for the ceremony. Later, Christine and Adam had a son and a daughter.

After Christine moved to Canada, she and Adam lived in an area with predominately German speaking families. Christine could not speak any English, but with the help of her friends she learned the language. They moved from Canada to Queens, New York. "Adam didn't want me to work, but I was determined to get a job. So, I put an ad in the newspaper, and I was hired by a nice Jewish lady." Christine worked cleaning house for a Jewish lady from Holland whose family had been killed in the war. "She was one of the best people in the world." Today, she and Adam speak German as well as English to each other at home.

JAPAN DURING WWII

Japan is a group of four main islands in the Pacific Ocean with the capital of Japan, Tokyo, on the largest island, Honshu. In the 1880's, many Japanese people came to the United States to work on the railroads and as farm laborers. According to the Library of Congress website, "More than 400,000 men and women left Japan for the United States. The two most popular destinations were the archipelago of Hawaii and America's Pacific northwest coast. In both places, the immigrants would discover a new and radically different way of life."

With Japan being a small island nation, it was looking for expansion for its large population during the late 1930's and 1940's. The leaders of Japan thought that invading China and French Indochina would give them the needed land and resources for their growing population.

Japan during the war~

Japan became part of the Axis powers of Japan, Germany, and Italy. In December 1941, Japan attacked Pearl Harbor bringing the United States into the war. The United States and Britain, along with Canada, Australia, and Cuba, formed the Allies. After four years of fighting, Japan surrendered on August 15, 1945, following the atomic bombing of Japanese cities Hiroshima and Nagasaki.

Japanese Americans in the United States

Once the United States entered WWII, many Americans became concerned the Japanese Americans living in the United States might still have an allegiance to their native country. So, all natural-born Japanese American people living in the United States were ordered to internment camps.

According to the website www.archive.vancouver.wsu.edu, "On February 19, 1942, President Franklin D. Roosevelt issued Executive Order 9066, which ordered the removal of 120,000 Japanese Americans from the West Coast to ten inland concentration camps located in isolated areas in seven states."

"The famous 442nd Regimental Combat team, made up entirely of Japanese Americans, became the war's most decorated unit." Some Japanese Americans were drafted as liaison soldiers to converse with the Japanese Prisoners of War and determine the Japanese officers' involvement in war crimes. After the surrender of Japan, the United States military occupied the country of Japan from 1945 to 1953.

Katherine N. Ase

How did WWII affect your life?

"Shortly after the bombing of Pearl Harbor in Hawaii, life changed radically for our family. On February 19, 1942,

Executive Order 9066 was signed by President Roosevelt. That act authorized the U.S. Army to expel all Japanese Americans living in the West Coast states of California, Oregon, Washington, and a part of Arizona. That spring the FBI came to our house unannounced, arrested my father without filing any charges, and jailed him. We did not see him again until January 1944."

"Before WWII, I lived in Niland, California, a small farming community about fifty miles from the United States-Mexican border. There were six of us in the family. I had two brothers and a sister. My parents were Japanese school teachers. Soon after the visit by the FBI, our usual activities were curtailed: a daylight curfew and limited travel were imposed, group meetings were banned, and bank accounts were frozen; however, we children were allowed to attend local schools. My sibs and I came home from school one day and found our house had been ransacked and our father gone."

"Later that spring, large posters were nailed to telephone posts in our neighborhood with instructions addressed to 'all persons of Japanese ancestry both alien and non-alien (US citizens)' regarding the planned expulsion from California. In May 1942, I became one of the 120,000 Japanese Americans who were forcibly removed from our homes. We were taken by bus to Poston, Arizona, and incarcerated in the large WRA (War Relocation Authority) camp which stood in a desolate desert without trees."

The Internment Camps in Arizona and Texas~

"The camp in Poston, Arizona, was organized into blocks with black tar-papered barracks for housing. Each block housed about 350 people. Our family of five was assigned a barren twenty by twenty-five-foot room. The walls adjoining our unit to the next did not reach the ceiling, so conversations could be heard. There were no cooking facilities, so all meals were eaten in the large mess hall. We used communal toilets, showers, and laundry tubs. We slept on iron cots with straw-filled mattresses. Soon, we curtained off the room into a sleeping and a living area. Adobe brick classrooms were hastily built to replace temporary buildings. We had Caucasian teachers from outside supplemented by internees living in the camp."

What were condition like in the camp?

"We used scrap lumber to make a table and some benches. There was no indoor heating or plumbing, so on cold winter days the men built outdoor bonfires for us. Most of the year the weather was very hot, dry, and there were frequent dust storms when strong winds blew over the desert. We nailed the tops of cans on the many knotholes to prevent dusty floors. We ate a lot of canned food until the camp farms began producing vegetables, poultry, tofu, and some other things."

"My mother worked in the diet kitchen in the hospital and my brother drove a van delivering supplies. Wages ranged from twelve to nineteen dollars a month. Most activities were held outdoors, so we walked to events and carried a stool. I remember going to baseball and basketball games and in winter carrying a tin pail filled with glowing charcoal to see old movies."

"On hot days, my brother and his friends would swim in the 'pool.' It was a large muddy dirt pit, filled with water. We walked everywhere since no one had a car: to church, classes, movies, the latrine, and the PX. We were confined in Poston for nineteen months, then released to move to another camp in Crystal City, Texas."

Pauline, Toyo, and Paul

Crystal City, Texas

"In January 1944, we went by train from Arizona to the DOJ (Department of Justice) camp. We had a joyful reunion with our father who had been released from a DOJ camp in Santa Fe, New Mexico. Housing provided for our family of six was a very compact prefab duplex. We shared the toilet with our neighbors. We used communal sinks, showers, and laundry tubs in the next block. My father worked in the bakery and my brother became the postman for the community. My other sibs and I attended school in the camp; the teachers were local Texans. We also joined sports teams and other youth activities."

"The camp was divided into a German section and a larger Japanese section. Parents were able to choose the school their children could attend – American, German, or Japanese. There were German families from the United States as well as from South America living in the camp. There were more Germans who came from South America while we lived there; however, there were very few compared to the Japanese American families settled in the camp."

What did you do after the war ended?

"After I graduated from high school in 1945, I worked for a few months in the camp hospital. The USPHS, United States Public Health Service, nurses influenced me to consider nursing. A former student contacted my mother and suggested a school in Minnesota. I applied and was admitted to Hamline-Asbury School of Nursing in Minneapolis in 1946. To acknowledge my Texas tan, my classmates soon dubbed me 'our sunburnt Swede.'"

Moving again~

"After we graduated from nursing school in 1949, Aileen, my roommate during our years in school, invited me to move to California with her family. She and I responded to an ad for two nurses in a doctor's office. When the staff at the office saw us, they decided the office only needed one nurse. My blonde friend Aileen's response was 'In that case we are not interested.' Both of us were hired right away at Los Angeles County Hospital. That summer Los Angeles was battling a polio epidemic. Aileen nursed patients in iron lungs, and I nursed patients who needed the constant application of hot packs, the Kenny Treatment."

According to Minnpost website, when Sister Kenny saw polio patients, "She thought the patients' limbs were stiff, not permanently paralyzed. She also was unaware of the accepted medical treatment. Instead of using braces to keep limbs rigid, she thought it was best to use hot packs and encourage gentle movement. Her method re-taught patients how to us limbs that had been only temporarily paralyzed by the virus."

The rest of my family after the war ended~

"My parents left Texas, relocated to Chicago, found work and lived in that city until they died in 1952 and 1978. My older brother was drafted in 1946 and served in the U.S. Army in Japan and Korea, until he died in 1955. My career in nursing has been challenging and satisfying. My younger brother became a chemist and my sister a physical therapist."

Joe Takehara, Pauline, Kate

World Health Organization

"In the 1970's, I was recruited by WHO as Nurse Educator to work at the College of Nursing in Mumbai and, subsequently, on a national manpower development project based in New Delhi, India. According to the Collins Dictionary website, "World Health Organization, or WHO, is responsible for helping governments to improve their health services. It is an agency of the United Nations."

What do you want America to know about your experiences?

"As a result, I was incarcerated for three and a half years, 1942-1945, in two different 'camps' in Arizona and Texas. The collective efforts of Japanese Americans to obtain Redress from the government was boosted after the 1993 report was issued by the Commission on Wartime Relocation and Internment of Civilians, or CWRIC. It stated that, 'The promulgation of Executive Order 9066 was not justified by military necessity, and the decision which followed it – detention, ending detention, and ending exclusion – were not driven by analysis of military conditions. The broad historical causes which shaped these decisions were race, prejudice, war hysteria, and a failure of political leadership.'"

"In 1990, as survivors, my brother, sister, and I were each given a letter of apology and a Redress check for twenty thousand dollars. In addition, Congress allotted funds for educating the public about that shameful time."

Anne Chieko Moore

Why did your parents come to the United States?

"My parents Shungo and Umeko Shimomura were from Kose and Takahashi, Okayama Prefecture in Japan. My father earned a degree in agriculture and my mother earned a degree in nursing from universities in Okayama City. They were both converted to Christianity by a missionary while they were students. They were the only Christians in either family. My father taught in a university before he immigrated to the United States to work in a Japanese labor camp. He returned to Japan, married my mother, and made the decision to strive for success at his own farm and provide a home for his wife in California. Soon after arriving in San Francisco, my father took my mother to be fitted for American clothes for the first time. My mother found some of these to be very uncomfortable and rather ridiculous looking but knew she should wear them instead of her kimono."

"Over the next twenty years, they moved several times in Salinas Valley, and my father gradually increased his farm and management responsibilities with financial success in raising sugar beets and head lettuce. Father and Mother provided a comfortable pleasant home for our active family of four sons and four daughters, all born in California. My father led the family with daily Bible reading and prayers. In addition to the household chores, my mother was sometimes called away to help Japanese mothers with the birth of babies. We often attended events at our church where my father served as elder for many years."

"My father had studied American history and was impressed with the ideals and accomplishments of the early leaders. He particularly admired Abraham Lincoln and named one of my brothers Lincoln. A pleasant memory of early years for me was Mother's bedtime stories, often retelling of old Japanese folktales. My parents spoke to us in Japanese; however, we siblings spoke to each other in English."

"In 1941, with optimistic expectations for the future, my father and mother decided to move to a 125-acre farm. Father filled the house with new furniture and appliances, purchased farm equipment, and a new car, and planted crops. The Caucasian farm owner, Mr. Bardin, and my father had some type of lease agreement through another party. Japanese immigrants were not permitted American citizenship or the right to buy property at this time."

How did WW II affect your life?

"Our family was shocked and appalled to hear of Japan bombing Pearl Harbor on December 7, 1941. Unfortunately, I was seven years old and had no idea what a Pearl Harbor was, but somehow understood some parts of the war as time passed by listening to the radio and conversations of grownups. My father and brothers hung black cloth over the windows for black out curtains. Sadly, while preparing to leave, my parents sorted through photos, documents, and letters and burned any items that might be incriminating."

"On February 19, 1942, President Franklin D. Roosevelt signed the Executive Order 9066, announcing that people of Japanese ancestry living on the West Coast were to be incarcerated. Lists of items we should take and those that would not be permitted were included on the posters which were posted on telephone poles and public buildings. We could take with us only what we could carry. Bank accounts were quickly frozen. Shoppers came to the farm to take away my father's farm equipment, for which he received no money."

"Mr. Bardin permitted us to store some of our possessions in a building on his farm, including the piano, the treadle Singer sewing machine, an armoire, some dishes and tools. We appreciated having these items shipped to us after the war was over. We were fortunate to have Mr. and Mrs. Bardin as kind and thoughtful friends. Just before we left, they brought lovely tiny gold heart shaped lockets with dainty chains for farewell gifts for my sister and me. It was heartening to have them with us while we were out in desolate surroundings. My parents protected us children by keeping us on the farm as much as possible to avoid abusive racist treatment of the public on the streets and in the stores. They also protected us by trying to avoid showing their concern and anxiety, so we were put to bed early."

Salinas Assembly Center – Rodeo ground Internment camp in California

"The assembly centers were required because the ten permanent camps were not completed. My family and I reported to Salinas Assembly Center (the rodeo grounds) on April 29, 1942. Mr. Bardin drove us there. The rodeo grounds were surrounded by high barbed wire fences. The entrance area was lined with young U.S. Army men, nervously gripping their rifles. Our family group trudging in together was reassuring to me, considering the unwelcoming entrance."

"One room or one fourth of a hastily built flimsy barrack of tarpaper walls on wooden frames provided living quarters for our family. Our only furniture were ten cots with our luggage crowding the room. There was one electric light bulb attached to a fixture in the center of the ceiling and no plumbing."

"In the morning, my mother took my younger sister and me to a horse trough to wash our faces and brush our teeth in cold water. My mother had bought us new towels, colorful toothbrushes with small animals hanging on the handles, and blue and white cans of Dr. West's tooth powder. And we were pleased. My mother had thoughtfully brought items to cheer us. The newly built outhouses had long rows of holes which were all the same size. I was afraid I would fall through the hole."

"Breakfast, lunch and supper were served at the mess hall for the block of about 300 people. We were told to bring our own unbreakable dishes and flatware. A large loud bell was rung when the meal was ready to be served. Most people arrived early and waited in lines. I remember some people complaining that they had to walk a long way, which was true if they lived at the opposite end of the block. I learned that the food budget was thirty-eight cents for three meals per person. I did not like the food."

"Heavy trucks brought supplies for building barracks, and it must have rained. There were muddy tracks everywhere. There was no school and sometimes some women called children to play together. Because the camp was for the Salinas area, my parents were pleased to visit with friends. My father was able to see a part of one of his former farm fields through the tall fence. My father continued daily Bible reading and prayers in our room. There was curfew starting around 8 p.m., and bright spotlights were turned on at the top of watch towers. After about three months, we were told to be ready to leave."

Poston Internment Camp in Arizona

"We were sent by train and bus to Poston Relocation Center

in Arizona which was on part of an Indian reservation on the sandy desert. Poston was one of the largest of the ten relocation centers and was divided into three camps housing 17,000 people. As at the Salinas Assembly Center, the barracks had wooden frames and black tarpaper for walls. Each barrack had four rooms, and although most families lived in one room, we had two rooms because there were ten of us. We were assigned to Camp 1, Block 32, Barrack 11, rooms B & C. On arrival that 100+ degree day, the boys and men in our family filled cotton bags with straw to be used as mattresses for our metal cots. Our family number was 13256, written on tags which were always attached to our clothing. There were over 300 people living in block 32, and our family seemed to be the only Christians there. Our Salinas area friends were all at Camp 2. My friendly mother helped us to get acquainted with our new neighborhood. Every evening my father continued our Bible reading and prayers at Poston."

"We were experienced with the mess hall facilities of Salinas when we arrived at Poston. After incarcerees began producing vegetables at the camps, the meals became more palatable. Some boys were always first in line and hungry, ate fast, wiped off their plates and leaped in line again for a second dinner. No one bothered to scold them."

"The lack of privacy in the latrines and showers without partitions was difficult, especially for women. However, I was so relieved to have flushing toilets instead of the outhouses of Salinas, and warm water for showers, I was not complaining."

"It was necessary for most of us to learn to adjust to the desert environment. Most residents from the Bay area were accustomed to 40 to 80-degree temperatures and suffered from the 100-degree heat. Many men wore small wet towels on their heads and women carried umbrellas. Dust storms were frequent and left behind one-inch layers of dust inside the barracks. The wind blew sand until it was impossible to see the building ahead of you. Scorpions, rattlesnakes, lizards, horned toads, black widow spiders, and large red ants were found in their desert environment, including in and around, the barracks. We were warned to shake our shoes before wearing because scorpions frequently wandered into them at night."

Working in the camp

"Some paid jobs were available in the camp. Monthly wages were twelve dollars, sixteen dollars, and nineteen dollars per person, according to the type of work. Physicians were the highest paid at nineteen dollars per month. My father worked as block janitor, my brother Taro operated heavy machinery to install roads, and my sister Toshi, fingerprinted incoming residents and was a typist at the administrative block office."

Medical facilities

"Some medical clinics were available but supplies and physicians were limited. Services and medicines for serious illnesses were difficult to provide. Physicians, nurses, and dentists were from the population of incarcerees. My mother was gone for several days for some kind of surgery, and I worried and wished someone had explained her illness. An older neighbor stayed with my sister and me during the day and taught me my first embroidery stitches."

School

"During the first year at Poston, school classes were held in a barrack room without most of the usual supplies. There were no desks: we each had a wooden crate to sit on, and any of my work was kept inside of it. There were no text books and little paper. Old magazines had been donated and these were used for many lessons, such as in looking for pictures that represent words. The teacher was a young Caucasian woman, perhaps a Quaker. She had her own textbook and a few other books. She also read to us. Teaching was a challenge under these circumstances."

"During that year, local men were recruited to make adobe bricks (for the sake of the children) and a school was built in time for the beginning of the next school year. The classrooms had black boards and a desk and a used textbook for each student. The wide cement walk at the edge of the building was a perfect place for a recess activity: playing with jacks that mothers had provided most girls, including me. Jacks and a ball in a cloth bag was my only toy my mother gave me to bring to camp."

Classes and activities

"After several months, administrators decided that adult classes would be helpful for the morale of the residents, so classes on many subjects were offered. My mother learned to make crepe paper flowers and wooden bird pins, studied English, and practiced Japanese brush calligraphy; and Father studied American history and English. My brothers found purpose and friendships in church activities. Wood scraps left over from building more barracks, window frames, and cabinets were secured from the trash piles and used for making many types of arts and crafts by the incarcerees. The

 hand carved wooden bird pins became popular in all the ten camps. Most of the people had never tried woodcarving birds, but the instructors were patient, kind, and encouraging. Although residents were not supposed to bring knives, most men had their pocket knives and lent them to women. The

men were more skilled than women at woodcarving and both painted well. By the time this activity was begun, residents were permitted to order sandpaper, pins, watercolors, and varnish from Montgomery Ward. The pleasant social interaction between the students and instructors was as important as the crafts. We, as a family, were proud of my mother and her lovely birds. Baseball became an important sport in all the camps and eventually camp teams of boys traveled long distances to compete. My favorite individual activity was making paper dolls from Corn Flakes boxes. Mother had packed pencils, crayons and scissors for us children. I had marvelous adventures with the paper dolls."

Military

"My oldest brother Taro was eighteen years old when he was drafted into the U.S. Army early in 1944. He was very angry about us being incarcerated and did not expect to survive the war. While he was being trained for a 442nd replacement in Florida, he was recruited to train for MIS in Minnesota because he was able to read Japanese that my mother had taught him at home. Obviously, my parents were sad when he left us from the Poston camp but rarely spoke of it to us. He was eventually sent to Japan and stayed until 1948. His absence left a large gap in the family group. More than 30,000 Japanese American men served in the U.S. Army during World War II."

Riots

"From the younger generation of Japanese American men came outbursts of anger that turned into riots, mostly in Camp 2, which led to severe punishment at Tule Lake Camp and deportation. Now years later, these men have been commended for fearlessly expressing complaints and anger for the incarceration, with courage, knowing of severe consequences to be endured."

Japanese culture

"Over all the ten incarceration camps, the majority of the incarcerees lived in a quiet controlled way which was given the term 'gaman', meaning self-restraint, patience, tolerance and endurance. My mother quietly insisted on 'gaman' in my behavior, meaning 'keep back tears' and 'don't complain'. There was no weeping in public areas although my mother told me later that she sometimes heard crying from other neighbors through the thin walls in our barrack, and she was also sometimes very sad."

Leaving the camp

"After two years in camp, my family was getting used to the odd way of living there, but my parents felt a need to try to start their lives again in a normal American setting as soon as we were permitted to leave. Taro was already serving in the Army. My sisters, Toshi and Sachi, left camp and tested Philadelphia as a possible place for the family. Now there were three gaps in the family circle. My sisters instructed my parents to move East. So, in six months we each received twenty-five dollars and took a five-day train ride to Philadelphia. I was happy to see my sisters. Mr. and Mrs. Patterson, of the War Relocation Authority, helped us to find a suitable work place for my father at an apple and peach farm in Riverton, New Jersey, owned by a Quaker couple, Mr. and Mrs. Sharpless Ritchee. They also provided a house for our family. My younger sister and I were given scholarships to attend Westfield Friends School for two years. The Quakers had been helpful to the incarcerees at the camps, providing advice and aid in many ways. Several of the teachers in Camp 1 were Quakers. The Ritchees welcomed us to New Jersey without knowing us. Later we moved outside Princeton where my father was employed at Princeton Nurseries."

"All eight of us siblings somehow completed college educations, which was important to our parents, even though they could not provide money for us. Due to the McCarren Walter Immigration and Naturalization Act of 1952, my parents became naturalized citizens in 1953, and proudly voted in the next election. Later, they bought their own house. After leaving camp, the incarceration was not discussed among my family members. Apparently, this was the occurrence among most of the camp incarcerees."

"The Redress campaign was begun in 1979 to seek reparations from the federal government for unjustly incarcerating us during World War II. President Jimmy Carter signed a bill to create a Commission of Wartime Relocation and Internment of Citizens. Following approval of House of Representatives and the Senate, President Reagan signed the Civil Liberty Act into law on April 11, 1988, requiring a letter of apology from the president and a payment of $20,000 to each survivor of the incarceration. My father was one of the 60,000 incarcerees who had died by then. We wish he could have known of this."

What do you want America to know about your experience?

"The incarceration of Japanese Americans was a serious violation of civil rights. We endured a forced internment of Japanese Americans because of racial prejudice and war hysteria in the United States. The success of the Redress campaign resulted in the Civil Liberties Act of 1988. With education and effort, the leaders of the government and the President of the United States can and will work to reverse wrong decisions and actions. So, in spite of us incarcerees being reticent to speak for ourselves, descendants among the following generations of Japanese Americans and other supporters provided historical education and persuasion to reverse the original Executive Order 9066 of 1942. There is no assurance that such action of racial prejudice will not be repeated, but there is hope that with education and dedicated interest in the welfare of the United States, the people will continue to influence our elected officials to work for justice for all, including minorities."

ROMANIA DURING WWII

Romania is in Europe west of the Soviet Union and surrounded by Hungary, Yugoslavia, and Bulgaria. After the fall of Poland, Romania lost much of its territories. The United States Holocaust Memorial Museum website states, "On November 20, 1940, Romania formally joined the Axis alliance." Even before Romania joined Nazi Germany, the authorities had a policy of persecution against the Jews.

The Iron Guard was a Fascist political group which was organized during this time period. Carol II, King of Romania, reigned from 1930 to 1940 and did not support the Iron Guard. According to the Britannica website, "In 1940, he was forced to abdicate in favor of his son Michael and to once again seek exile."

According to the *History Channel*, "On this day October 7, 1940, Hitler occupied Romania as part of his strategy of creating an unbroken Eastern front to menace the Soviet Union."

Romania and the Jewish people~

From the early nineteen thirties, there was an anti-Semitic feeling in Romania. Jews were banned from attending certain events; Jewish lawyers had their licenses revoked; and the Romanian citizenship of Jews was cancelled. Many Jewish Romanians who were living in villages were murdered or deported. Jewish families were forced to go to concentration camps in Germany. Eva Kor, a Holocaust survivor, and her family were sent to Auschwitz from their village in Romania. Eva said, "WWII definitely removed me from a little naïve girl in a peaceful village. Even that peaceful village became a center of harassment, abuse, and discrimination once the Nazis took over."

Romania changes sides~

"By the time that Romania broke with Nazi Germany and entered the war on the side of the Allies (August 23, 1944), Romanian Jewry had considerably decreased." (www.jewishvirtuallibrary.org)

Eva Mozes Kor

Eva was one of the two hundred surviving twins who were used in experiments at the hands of the Nazis. Eva's family was the only Jewish family in her village, and in March 1944, Eva and her family were forced from their home to the Cehei Ghetto. In May 1944, they were taken by train to Auschwitz. She and her sister, Miriam, spent about nine months in the camp. Eva and Miriam were about ten years old at the time they were sent to Auschwitz. "The beatings by my father helped me to be strong and smart. I was able to survive the Nazis." Dr. Mengele was responsible for the medical problems that Miriam experienced later in life. Auschwitz concentration camp was liberated on January 27, 1945.

"As a ten-year old child, I thought the whole world was a concentration camp. I thought everyone else lived like I lived: without parents, starving to death and surrounded by Nazi guards. One day there was a plane flying very low over the camp; I could see the American flag on one of the wings. How did I know about the American flag? I had an aunt in Cleveland, Ohio, who sent us letters. On the letters were stamps that had the American flag on them. That is how I knew what the American flag looked like. It was a big discovery for me that the Americans were coming to free us. By November the number of airplanes increased, and all the experiments stopped. In my mind, I am thinking I don't want to be near the Germans when they are winning the war, so I don't want to be near them when they are losing the war." So many people lost their lives so near the end of the war when the Nazis were trying to get rid of the evidence of their crimes.

Liberation

One day Eva woke up, and "It was eerily quiet. A woman came into the barracks and said, 'We are free, we are free, we are free!' We saw men in white camouflage suits. I didn't know who they were, but the important part was Miriam and I were alive. I couldn't believe it. My first taste of freedom was chocolate, hugs, and cookies. It was the Soviet Army that liberated Auschwitz."

Eva and Miriam leave Auschwitz.

After Eva and Miriam were freed from the concentration camp, they spent some time in refugee camps. Eva's mother, father and two of her sisters died at the hands of the Nazis. She asked, Mrs. Csengeri, another survivor at the camp, to sign some papers saying she was their aunt. "I wanted to go home to Romania. She took Miriam and me out of the orphanage and cleaned us of lice and made little dresses out of Army shirts for us. We stayed with her for the next nine months. We arrived in Romania in November 1945. When I approached our house, it looked neglected and like no one was at home. It had been ransacked and was empty. I found three crumpled pictures on the bedroom floor. I picked them up and put them in my pocket. I never looked at the pictures until 1978. I could not cope with my past."

"In 1946, the Communist took over Romania, and I joined the Communist party in 1948." Eva was fourteen years old and living with a surviving aunt. She did not like being a Communist and applied for an exit visa to leave Romania. "I was not a good Communist," said Eva. "Originally, the Communists said we could take the things that we had collected since leaving the camp with us. By 1950, when the visa was issued, they said we could only take the clothes on our back. We were the last transport to leave Romania to go to Israel. The Russians closed down the borders for ten years."

She has been lecturing about the Holocaust, Dr. Mengele, Auschwitz, and forgiveness for nearly forty years. At one time, Eva spoke seven languages; however, it has been some time since she has spoken some of them. She said, "not so many now." One of the things that she wanted to emphasize was: "Forgiveness equals seed for peace; Anger equals seed for war. Hitler was a very angry man."

Eva and Miriam had an aunt in Cleveland, Ohio, and she sent some material to the girls for dresses. The girls were living with another aunt and uncle in Israel. Eva and Miriam arrived in Israel when they were sixteen and spent two years living and going to school on an agricultural farm. At age eighteen, they were conscripted into the Israel Defense Forces where Eva studied drafting and Miriam studied nursing. She still recalls this thought, "I can do something to remove the focus from me."

Eva meets Michael~

Michael (Mickey) Kor, a Holocaust survivor, who was liberated by the Americans, told the American troops, "You Americans are very nice; I would like to come to America." In 1946, he moved to the United States. In 1960, Michael came to Israel on vacation to visit his brother. Eva went out with Michael on a blind date and opted to marry him. So, they left Tel Aviv and moved to Terre Haute, Indiana.

CANDLES Museum~

"I donated my left kidney to Miriam on November 16, 1987. A year after the transplant Miriam developed cancer. Miriam died on June 6, 1993." Eva opened CANDLES Museum in honor of Miriam in 1995. CANDLES is the acronym for *Children of Auschwitz Nazi Deadly Lab Experiments Survivors.* The museum is in Terre Haute, Indiana, and has as its focus to educate people about the Holocaust.

How did WWII affect your life?

Other than the fact that she lost her family due to the Nazis and WWII, Eva replied with the following statement. "WWII removed me from a peaceful village and put me in a place that was exempt from many things that people take for granted. There was nothing there that resembled normal human existence in my opinion. Everything was crazy. That was the environment in which I ended up. The only reason I survived was because I got a lot of training from my father."

What do you want America to know about your experiences?

"When I was in Auschwitz, I was scared but I never gave up on myself. I am very happy to be alive. Forgive your worst enemy. It will set you free. Forgiveness is the best revenge. Also, forgiveness is self-liberating and self-empowering. It has no side effects. I forgive the Nazis."

Was there anything funny in your experience during the war?

"When I was a little girl, we used to have plays. We performed them in our backyard with our cousins. The neighbors and relatives would watch. Whenever I said something funny, the people would laugh. When I was a little girl, I wanted to be a comedian; somehow my destiny sent me in the wrong direction. So, my life is not that funny. I do use humor to relieve stress in my talks."

What was your greatest achievement in your life?

"I learned to like who I am. There were different steps that I had to do. I never liked myself when I lived in Europe. Even after the war the Jews were persecuted by the Communists. When I lived in Israel, I went to bed at night hoping I would wake up and no one would take me away or hurt me because I was Jewish. You have to like who you are because you cannot be anybody else but yourself. You have to have positive experiences that relate to who you are. That was what I got from Israel. I love who I am even though I am Jewish. That is very important."

Eva Kor today ~

Eva is often featured in the Indianapolis Star updating the community on what she is doing. There was a documentary of her life titled, *Eva*, which premiered April 2018. It was narrated by actor Ed Asner and featured several other well-known personalities – former NBA player Ray Allen, actor Elliott Gould, and CNN journalist Wolf Blitzer. Also, Eva has written three books, *Surviving the Angel of Death*, *Echoes from Auschwitz*, and *Little Eva and Miriam in First Grade*.

In April 2017, Eva was awarded the 2017 Sachem Award by Indiana Governor Eric Holcomb. According to Governor Holcomb's office, the Sachem Award is given "to recognize a lifetime of excellence and moral virtue that has brought credit and honor to Indiana." It is only awarded to one person each year.

Conclusion

The fifty-five women who were interviewed in this book represent the military, medical personnel, Holocaust survivors, factory workers, Rosie the Riveters, young girls, and everyday housewives. The contributions of all the women represented in this book are a testament to the fortitude of the American woman during wartime.   The common thread that ran through many of their stories was "we are all in this together" and "this is what I can do for the war effort." Without all the people in the nation working together there may have been a different ending to the WWII story.

These women revealed information about their life during the days of the 1940's when they were young women, teenagers, or children. In some cases, they had to endure hardships and life changing situations.   These unforgettable stories are in their own words and demonstrate how strong these women were and how their WWII sacrifices shaped their future decisions.

Acknowledgements

Thomas Brinduse	proofreading, encouragement
Ruby Hardy	coordinator of California stories
C Ray Minton Jr.	proofreading, patience
Diane Meier	editing and proofreading
Rebecca Osher	encouragement, information
Amy Pitcher	book formatting, editing, and technical support
Marcelle Randolph	proofreading
Brenda Serensky	proofreading

Dedicated to a special man for his service to America

Ralph Cooley – U.S. Army
February 9, 1927 - April 19, 2018

Liam & Noah Pitcher, Ralph, Lillie & Evan Cooley

Bibliography

Websites

1. www.amhistory.si.edu. *The Price of Freedom: American Red Cross Uniforms*. Accessed August 10, 2018

2. www.amp.theguardian.com, *The Guardian Obituary for Lettice Curtis*. Accessed March 25, 2018

3. www.amp.theguardian.com, *Is this Bush's Secret Bunker?* Tom Vanderbilt, Monday, August 28, 2006. Accessed June 19, 2018

4. www.atomicheritage.org, Atomic Heritage Foundation, Accessed August 20, 2018

5. www.baleinsendirect.org, *Are There Any Whales that Live in Fresh Water?* Whales Online, February 12, 2015 Par Marie-Sophie Giroux. Accessed September 6, 2018

6. www.biography.com/people/jacquelinecochran. Last updated August 20, 2015. Accessed July 12, 2018

7. www.britannica.com, Adrian Gilbert. Accessed March 26, 2018

8. www.britannica.com, Iron Guard, Romanian Organizations, Carol II King of Romania, Accessed July 31, 2018

9. www.capeelizabeth.com, *History of Ft. Williams.* Accessed December 21, 2017

10. www.cnn.com/2015/8/31/china, *Forgotten Ally? China's Unsung Role in WWII.* Updated August 31, 2015. Rana Mitter, Special to CNN. Accessed July 30, 2018

11. www.collinsdictionary.com, World Health Organization. Accessed July 12, 2018

12. www.content.time.com, *Madame Chiang Kai-Shek 1898-2003* Tony Karon, Friday, October 24, 2003. Accessed July 31, 2018

13. www.France-Pub.com, *Second World War in France.* Accessed July 28, 2018

14. www.globalsecurity.org, *Panama Canal – Defending the Canal.* Accessed April 30, 2018

15. www.guides.harvard.edu, *Nursing and the Red Cross – World War II.* Research Guides at Harvard University

16. www.history.com, German Troops Enter Romania. Accessed July 31, 2018

17. www.history.com, *American Women During WWII,* Eleanor Roosevelt. Accessed August 14, 2018

18. www.history.com, *Japanese Internment Camps,* Accessed July 28, 2018

19. www.histclo.com.ww2.cou.ger.welfare, *World War II – German Red Cross* Deutsches Rotes Kreuz. December 17, 2009. Updated January 17, 2017. Accessed August 9, 2018

20. www.history-state.gov, *Lend-Lease and Military Aid to the Allies in the Early Years of World War II,* Milestones: 1937-1945. Accessed July 29, 2018

21. www.historycentral.com, USS *Whitney,* Whitney AD-4, Accessed December 21, 2017

22. www.historylearningsite.co.uk, *The French Resistance.* History Learning Site, Updated 18 May 2015. C N Trueman. Accessed July 28, 2018

23. www.historynet.com, History Net. *Grumman F4F Wildcat: U.S. Navy Fighter in World War II* by Bruce L. Crawford, June 12, 2006. Accessed April 26, 2018

24. www.homefrontheroines.com. Accessed April 3, 2018

25. www.in.gov, IHB: Freeman Field. Accessed November 25, 2017

26. www.independent.co.uk. *Lettice Curtis.* Accessed September 3, 2018.

27. www.indystar.com, *Holocaust Survivor Eva Kor,* robert.king@indystar.com, December 29, 2017. Accessed March 25, 2018

28. www.indystar.com, Robert King, December 30, 2017. Accessed March 26, 2018

29. www.indystar.com, Dawn Mitchell, *What happened to 'Omar Man'?* March 11, 2018. Accessed March 11, 2018.

30. www.indystar.com, Obituaries – Sophie Lee Woo. Accessed September 2, 2018

31. www.indystar.com, Kristen Jordan Shamus, Detroit Free Press. Accessed March 26, 2018

32. www.insideindianabusiness.com/story/34724397/state -names-schem-awad-winner, *State Names Sachem Award Winner.* Updated March 10, 2017. Accessed November 4, 2017.

33. www.iwm.org.uk/history/9-iconic-aircraft. Ian Carter, Friday 5 January 2018. 9 *Iconic Aircraft from the Battle of Britain.* Accessed March 26, 2018

34. www.loc.gov, Japanese – Introduction Immigration. Accessed August 19, 2018

35. www.med-dept.com/articles/ww2-hospital-ships. Accessed August 18, 2018

36. www.merriam-webster.com/dictionary. Accessed July 15, 2018

37. www.militaryfactory.com/aircraft/detail, updated February 21, 2018, authored by staff writer. Accessed March 26, 2018

38. www.nytimes.com, The New York Times, Margalit Fox, January 22, 1018. Daniel E. Slotnik, contributed reporting, *Naomi Parker Fraley, The Real Rosie the Riveter, Dies at 96.* Accessed July 23, 2018

39. www.nytimes.com, archive, April 19,1945, *Ernie Pyle is Killed on Ie Island; Foe Fired When All Seemed Safe.* Accessed June 18, 2018

40. www.nytimes.com, *Madam Chiang, 105, Chinese Leader's Widow, Dies.* Seth Faison, October 24, 2003. Updated November 17, 2003. Accessed July 31, 2018

41. www.redcross.org, "Red Cross Services to the Armed Forces: Then & Now." Posted November 10, 2014. Accessed August 9, 2018

42. www.reminisce.com, June/July 2018. David Neal Keller, Dublin, OH. Accessed August 10, 2018

43. www.revolvy.com, Festung. Accessed July 15, 2018

44. www.usautoindustrywrldwartwo.com, *Marmon-Herrington in World War Two, The American Automobile Industry in World War Two,* David D. Jackson. Updated June 28, 2018. Accessed July 19, 2018

45. www.ushmm.org, United States Holocaust Memorial Museum, Romania. Accessed July 31, 2018

46. www.uso.org, Accessed July 21, 2018

47. www.ww2db.com, *Burma Road and the Hump*, WWII Database, 1 January 1938 - 10 November 1945. David Stubblebine. Accessed July 31, 2018

48. www.warfarehistorynetwork.com, *The Abwehr's Man in Havana*, Peter Kross. Accessed July 27, 2018

49. www.wordpress.com, *Kings Bay/Georgia and World War II*, Accessed December 5, 2017

50. www.worldwartwo.net, *Barrage Balloons // World War Two*, Source: Aerospace Power Journal – Summer 1989, The Official Web Site of the 225th AAA Searchlight Battalion Veterans Association. Accessed July 29, 2018

51. www.yosemite.epa.gov. *Hanford, Washington – Nuclear site*. Last updated November 16, 2017. Accessed November 24, 2018

Books

1. *Allison War Album*, General Motors, Indianapolis, Indiana, circa 1945

2. Cobblestone, December 1985, Volume 6 Number 12. Page 44. Franklin D. Roosevelt Library, World War II: The Home Front.

3. *MacArthur At War: World War II in the Pacific*, Borneman, Walter R., Little, Brown & Co. May 2016

Museums

1. Imperial War Museum, Duxford Airfield, Cambridge CB2 4QR